During Wind and Rain

THE UNITED STATES OF AMERICA,

CERTIFICATE
No. 6308

To all to whom these Presents shall come, Greeting:

WHEREAS *Uriah Jones of Arkansas County, Arkansas Assignee of Pha-nubbee.*

ha *s* deposited in the GENERAL LAND OFFICE of the United States, a Certificate of the REGISTER OF THE LAND OFFICE at *Little Rock, Arkansas* whereby it appears that Choctaw Certificate *6308* in the name of *Pha-nubbee.* for *One hundred and Sixty* acres of land, (issued by the Secretary of War in pursuance of the provisions of the Act of Congress of the 23d of August, 1842, entitled, "An Act to provide for the satisfaction of claims arising under the fourteenth and nineteenth Articles of the Treaty of Dancing Rabbit Creek, concluded in September, one thousand eight hundred and thirty."— of the Act of Congress of the 3d of March, 1845, entitled, "An Act making appropriations for the current and contingent expenses of the Indian Department, and for fulfilling treaty stipulations with the various Indian tribes for the fiscal year, commencing on the 1st day of July, 1845, and ending on the 80th day of June, 1846," and of the Joint Resolution of Congress of the 3d August, 1846, entitled, "Joint Resolution to authorize the Secretary of War to adjudicate the claims of the Su-quak-natch-ah and other clans of Choctaw Indians, whose cases were left undetermined by the Commissioners for the want of the Township maps") has been surrendered by the said *Uriah Jones* in full satisfaction for *the North East Quarter of Section Thirteen, in Township Nine South, of Range Three West. in the District of Lands subject to Sale at Little Rock, Arkansas. containing One hundred and Sixty Acres.*

according to the official plat of the survey of the said Lands, returned to the General Land Office by the SURVEYOR GENERAL, which said Tract has been located by the said *Uriah Jones.*

NOW, KNOW YE, That the United States of America, in consideration of the premises, and in conformity with the several Acts of Congress, in such case made and provided, HAVE GIVEN AND GRANTED, and by these presents DO GIVE AND GRANT, unto the said *Uriah Jones.*

and to *his* heirs, the said tract above described: TO HAVE AND TO HOLD the same, together with all the rights, privileges, immunities and appurtenances, of whatsoever nature thereunto belonging, unto the said

Uriah Jones and to *his* heirs and assigns forever.

In Testimony Whereof, I, *Zachary Taylor,*

PRESIDENT OF THE UNITED STATES OF AMERICA, have caused these Letters to be made PATENT, and the SEAL of the GENERAL LAND OFFICE to be hereunto affixed.

GIVEN under my hand, at the CITY OF WASHINGTON, the *First* day of *August* in the year of our Lord one thousand eight hundred and *forty nine* and of the INDEPENDENCE OF THE UNITED STATES the seventy- *fourth*

BY THE PRESIDENT: *Z Taylor.*

By *Th. Ewing Jr.* Asst. Sec'y.

N Sargent RECORDER of the General Land Office.

Recorded Vol. *1* , page *367.*

During Wind and Rain

The Jones Family Farm
in the Arkansas Delta, 1848–2006

MARGARET JONES BOLSTERLI

The University of Arkansas Press
Fayetteville
2008

ISBN-10: 1-55728-871-2
ISBN-13: 978-1-55728-871-4

12   11   10   09   08   5   4   3   2   1

Designed by Liz Lester

♾ The paper used in this publication meets the minimum requirements of the
American National Standard for Permanence of Paper for Printed Library Materials
Z39.48-1984.

LIBRARY OF CONGRESS CATALOGING-IN-PUBLICATION DATA

Bolsterli, Margaret Jones.
    During wind and rain : the Jones family farm in the Arkansas Delta,
  1848-2006 / Margaret Jones Bolsterli.
        p.   cm.
    Companion vol. to: Born in the Delta.
    Includes bibliographical references and index.
    ISBN-13: 978-1-55728-871-4 (pbk. : alk. paper)
    ISBN-10: 1-55728-871-2 (pbk. : alk. paper)
      1. Jones family. 2. Bolsterli, Margaret Jones—Family. 3. Farm life—
  Arkansas—Desha County—History. 4. Family farms—Arkansas—Desha
  County—History. 5. Desha County (Ark.)—Social life and customs. 6. Desha
  County (Ark.)—Biography. 7. Arkansas Delta (Ark.)—Social life and customs.
  8. Arkansas Delta (Ark.)—Biography. I. Bolsterli, Margaret Jones. Born in the
  Delta. II. Title.
      F417.D4B655   2008
      976.7´85—dc22

                                                    2007048834

For the Descendants of
Uriah and Sarah Jones

During Wind and Rain

They sing their dearest songs—
He, she, all of them—yea,
Treble and tenor and bass,
    And one to play;
With the candles mooning each face. . . .
    Ah, no; the years O!
How the sick leaves reel down in throngs!

They clear the creeping moss—
Elders and juniors—aye,
Making the pathways neat
    And the garden gay;
And they build a shady seat. . . .
    Ah, no; the years, the years;
See, the white storm-birds wing across!

They are blithely breakfasting all—
Men and maidens—yea,
Under the summer tree,
    With a glimpse of the bay,
While pet fowl come to the knee. . . .
    Ah, no; the years O!
And the rotten rose is ript from the wall.

They change to a high new house,
He, she, all of them—aye,
Clocks and carpets and chairs
    On the lawn all day,
And brightest things that are theirs. . . .
    Ah, no; the years, the years;
Down their carved names the rain-drop ploughs.

THOMAS HARDY

CONTENTS

ILLUSTRATIONS

Throughout my childhood, there were three trunks in our house on the farm in the Arkansas/Mississippi Delta. One was a small tin trunk brought by my grandmother, Mary Margaret Brown, when she came as a bride to the home of my grandfather, Joseph H. Jones, in about 1870. In it were legal papers having to do with their generation as well as some concerning his father, Uriah, and scraps of information concerning her own family, the Ira E. Brown family of Maury County, Tennessee. Since the information in her trunk was seldom needed anymore, it was stored in a dark attic, out of the way but safe. In my Aunt Sallie's bedroom there stood a large, rectangular, cloth-covered trunk in which she kept her treasures: an old fox neckpiece, odds and ends of jewelry, a hank of her hair cut when she was young, letters, photographs, the family Bible, and legal papers concerning her tenure as owner of the remnant of the farm my great-grandfather Uriah had started putting together in 1849. In my parents' bedroom there was an identical trunk containing my mother's treasures and legal papers concerning my father's tenure as the farmer while it was Aunt Sallie's land and then when it belonged to him. When Aunt Sallie died in 1936, her trunk was moved upstairs, contents undisturbed, except that the Jones family Bible was moved to the trunk belonging to my mother, who took charge of the family record of births, marriages, and deaths.

In about 1980, my sister Pauline Lloyd, who was living in the house, asked me to go through the trunks and sift out anything that ought to be saved. I think she was worried about fire and the possible loss of anything of value to the family. I put the things I thought might be useful or at least interesting someday in a large box and asked my brother Grover to keep it until called for, as I was about to go to Connecticut for a year and would be leaving strangers in my house. He put the box on a shelf in his laundry room, and I forgot about it. In about 1985, I happened to remember it while down there on a visit and brought it back to Fayetteville and put it on a shelf in my study.

From there it was transferred to a shelf in my study on a farm in Madison County a friend and I had moved to in 1987 and was forgotten again.

And then—it must have been about 1996—after my retirement from the University of Arkansas, I was sitting at my desk one day and noticed it staring me in the face from across the room. I opened the box and was stunned at the rich deposit of information about my family and the struggle they had made to hang onto the farm over the course of 145 years. I had always known things had been difficult, for I had, after all, grown up during the Great Depression and had heard stories about the Civil War, Reconstruction, and the 1927 Flood. But I had no idea of how hard it had really been from 1861 to about 1937 until I saw it documented there in black and white, time and again, on legal papers threatening foreclosures and on the mortgages taken out to pay the few dollars owed in taxes that stopped the forfeiture proceedings. Even sadder, of course, were the notices when the proceedings had not been stopped and land was lost.

Those three trunks had contained the family archives, and every scrap of paper was revered. There were old gin tickets, bills of lading for things shipped on steamboats to market in Memphis, and receipts for purchases made there. There were mortgage papers, tax receipts, and all manner of legal papers that had been kept in case they might be needed. There were doctor bills for fatal illnesses from 1903 that were still being talked about in 1940 as if they had happened the year before. There was the receipt for the purchase of my father's first automobile. There were pocket notebooks that my grandfather and father carried daily to record everything they needed to remember. There were some neatly kept accounts ledgers from my father's and my brother Grover's tenures as farmer. Letters from friends and family members who had moved away as well as records from the family Bible of births, deaths, and marriages were preserved so that the private side of the family's lives could be documented there as well as in the public records. That cardboard box held a world of information begging to be explored, but I still did nothing about it because I could not figure out a way to combine the family's story with that of the land. I had already published a memoir, *Born in the Delta:*

Reflections on the Making of a Southern White Sensibility, about my childhood on our farm and the culture that shaped us and did not want to repeat what I had told there.

I wanted to do something else, but I did not understand what until 1997, when the Program in Agrarian Studies at Yale University gave me a fellowship and a glorious year there in which to think about agricultural history. Every Friday the fellows met to discuss a paper that somehow or other, in some way, touched agrarian life, and over the course of that year I began to see a way to explore the two narratives that were intertwined here: one of the family and its struggle and the other of the land and the way it was worked over a period of some 150 years, as the farming methods changed from handwork and mule work to something akin to mechanized engineering. My opportunity for exploration was special in that I not only had the family papers for documentation but also the family stories and memories to draw on, for the dream of the farm and what it meant was my dream as well. In addition, I had at my disposal the living memories of my sister Pauline Lloyd, who has lived on the farm all but some fifteen of her ninety years, and my brothers Jodie and Bob Jones, who actually did some of the work in the fields that I describe and speak from experience that I, being female, never was afforded.

Conditioned as we are by Laura Ingalls Wilder's version of life on the northwestern frontier, we must be cautioned to remember that life on other frontiers took different shapes, according to the topography and soil. In the Arkansas Delta, life on the family farm, what one might think of as the "Little House in the Swamp," may have had some similarities to a homestead in Wisconsin, but the nature of the ideals and expectations brought to it made it different from the very beginning from the "Little House on the Prairie." This Delta farm was hacked out of the woods in the 1840s by slaves who became sharecroppers in 1865, some of whose descendants were tractor drivers in the 1960s. In other words, ours was a farm managed like a plantation because the plantation ideal that was central to the vision of the farm's founder has been, to some extent, carried on down to the present. It was a *farm* because it was too small to be termed a *plantation* (not for lack of trying.) One difference was that, in this scheme of things, white women of a certain class did not work in the fields nor did they cook huge meals for hungry harvesting crews. They were kept on as high a pedestal as the family could afford. The culture produced by this ideal was my theme in *Born in the Delta,* so I will not belabor it here except to make the point again that these pioneers probably did not consider their venture a matter of *going West,* with its connotations of wide open spaces and freedom to build a new kind of life, but of moving the boundary of the *South* further west. They wanted their lives to be as much as possible like the ones left behind in Virginia and Tennessee, or like the lives they would have preferred to have back there. The egalitarian dream that descendants of Texans—and others who went further west—claim for their forebears was not their priority. In any case, one suspects that the further west settlers went, the harder it was to retain the Southern ideals, no matter how much they might have wanted to. The western border of Arkansas may have been about as far as those ideals could thrive. Observers attest to the difficulty of achieving them in east Texas, as in this letter written by Venable Daniel from Mckinney, Texas, back to his family in North Carolina in September 1866:

> There is less attention paid here to the gradation of society than any where I have ever been. There seems nothing here to form an aristocracy: if a man gives a party here everybody comes without an invitation except the ladies are generally invited. The daughter of the Governor will dance at a party with a shoe maker, a house carpenter or a merchant alike. Governor Throckmorton the recent gov. elect lives three miles from here; every one calls him "Jim" from the ox driver to the lawyer.[1]

Society was not this relaxed in Dallas County, Arkansas, some sixty miles away from the Jones farm, where Bailey Bullock, future sister-in-law of Mr. Daniel, was growing up on a plantation also settled in 1849 while remaining absorbed, as completely as possible, with the social norms of North Carolina.[2] The cultural differences were still noticeable in 1947 to Shirley Abbott, who grew up in Hot Springs, Arkansas, and went to college that year at Texas State College for Women in Denton, Texas, which she characterizes as being on the cusp of Southern and Western cultures.

About half the students were Southerners from Louisiana and
Arkansas and Mississippi, as well as the farm country of East
Texas (with a few city girls from Houston and Dallas mixed in.),
but the rest were Texans from the high plains and were notice-
ably different from the rest of us. They were a wilder, stronger
breed; beside them we Southerners looked positively dainty.
They were unfeminized. They had no interest in clothes, wore
their hair cropped, slept late on Sunday mornings while we were
putting on our pretty little hats and waiting for the bus to go to
Sunday School. . . . They all played golf and tennis, fenced like
masters and had won their life-saving badges, apparently, while
still in grammar school. I was frightened to death of them, but
I envied them, too, because along with their life-saving badges,
they seemed to have earned some magic exemption from the
fate the college clearly had in mind for most of us: it wanted to
turn us Southern girls into Southern ladies.[3]

The recognition of a fairly rigid caste system and the encouragement of patriarchy with protected and powerless roles for white
women was certainly one of the characteristics of culture in the frontier houses in the swamps of Arkansas and Mississippi, and it was linked
to others, especially to the all-encompassing hope of building a farming enterprise so successful that the owner and his family would never
have to work in the fields themselves. The plantation was the model
here, not the "family farm" where everyone in the family worked to
get the crop planted and harvested. It might be accurate to say that
the ideal here was a "factory farm" from the very beginning.

I have tried to shape this book as a companion volume to *Born
in the Delta,* relating here our hopes and fears to the actual farming
of the land. For the family that saw hacking this farm out of the
wilderness as a good reason to stop on the great road west is still
there. And since it is my family, I hope to tell about it from a special perspective, being privy to the hopes and aspirations passed
down in our stories—our myths and legends, certified by those
papers squirreled away in the attic by successive generations chron-
icling the struggles to hang onto the land and to prevail as farmers
through times that would have tried anybody's soul.

One farmer in each of five generations has taken the operation through changes in method—from the use of slaves with hoes and primitive plows, to a long period of sharecropping with somewhat less primitive tools, and on down to the present with its salaried drivers on tractors with disks that work eight rows at a time and cultivate an acre in five minutes and its catfish ponds dug out of the richest land in the world.

In lieu of papers from the trunks that I relied on for earlier generations, I have been helped in documenting the last phase of this enterprise by conversations with my nephew Casey Jones, the farmer in the fifth generation, and through access to the detailed records of his daily farm operations from 1980 until 1995 that make it possible to estimate the differences between yields in 1860 and 2004 for some of the same fields. Moreover, without his careful notation of the steps necessary to raise a crop during the last twenty-five years, it might not be possible to imagine the almost overwhelming scope of the changes in methods made possible by advances in technology. My brother Jodie's written account of the process of field work in the 1930s and '40s serves the same function for that period of time, and I appreciate his permission to quote it at such length. My thanks go as well to my nephew Billy Lloyd and his friends Bob Spainhouer and Wayne Smith for their help in tracking down information in Desha County during the last days of research there.

I am grateful for the memories shared with me by my sister Pauline and brothers Jodie and Bob and for their encouragement in this endeavor, and I am indebted as always to my sons Eric and David for their support.

The most persistent help has come, as usual, from Olivia Sordo, Willard B. Gatewood, and Hilary Harris, who read this manuscript in several drafts, made useful suggestions, and convinced me that the project should be completed. Indeed, I might not have seen it through without their sometimes relentless encouragement. I was also especially fortunate to have had the sensitive, detailed suggestions of the two readers chosen by the University of Arkansas Press to evaluate this manuscript. Jane Adams and Grey Osterud went far beyond the call of duty in guiding me towards the final draft, and I deeply appreciate the trouble they took.

CHAPTER I

The Place They Came To

The Arkansas/Mississippi Delta

In 1841, my great-grandparents, Uriah Jones, his wife Sarah and their small son Joseph, who was to become my grandfather, moved west from central Tennessee to Arkansas County, Arkansas, in the Arkansas/Mississippi Delta. In August 1849, as assignee of a Choctaw Indian named Pha-Nubbee, Uriah presented a patent for 160 acres of land at the General Land Office in Little Rock and received title to the "northeast quarter of section 13, township 9S, range 3 W," situated in Redfork Township, Desha County, Arkansas, the adjacent new county to the south. On November 1 of the same year, he bought an adjoining tract from the government, "The North East Quarter of the North West Quarter of Section Thirteen in Township Nine South, of Range three West in the district of lands subject to sale at Little Rock, Arkansas, containing Forty Acres."[1] According to the text on it, Choctaw Certificate #630B for the 160-acre plot of land had been awarded to Pha-Nubbee by an act of Congress in 1842 to satisfy claims arising from the fourteenth and nineteenth articles of the Treaty of Dancing Rabbit Creek of 1830, the treaty that initiated the removal of the Five Civilized Tribes to the west. It is not known where Uriah came by it nor how much he paid for it—there was a thriving market in these certificates. Nor is it

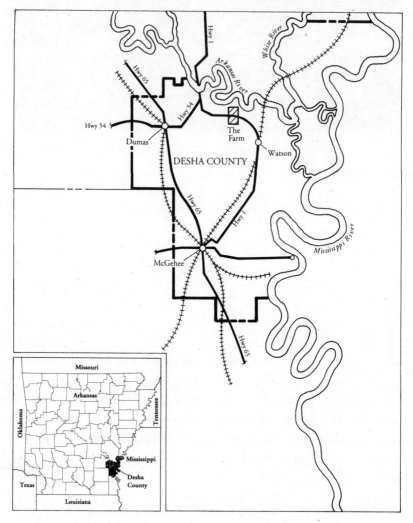

Contemporary map of Desha County showing roads, railroads, towns and rivers.

known whether this particular Indian ever saw the property, but evidence of Native American tenure was still around as late as 1940 or so in mounds, now leveled, that stood just above the northeast boundary of the farm and in relics still being turned up by plows. His second purchase, the additional 40-acre plot, was sold by the government in compliance with an act of Congress in April 24, 1820.

This plot of two hundred acres became the core of the farm that has sustained some of our family for seven generations, our pot of gold at the end of the western rainbow. Over the years the family has bought, sold, lost, and been given other acreage in the neighborhood, but some of this original land has belonged to some of us and been the center of most of our imaginations for 150 years. The story of this farm, the people it nurtured, and their struggle to hang onto it is a tale in microcosm of the successful westward migration in the United States of America. It is also a story of the relationship between people and the land during their long engagement in a particular type of farming. Theirs was one version of the American dream. Anyone who thinks making America was easy should reflect on the experiences noted here.

When Uriah laid claim to his property in 1849, he was employed as overseer on a large plantation adjacent to his land belonging to George W. Martin of Davidson County, Tennessee, near Nashville. Martin had bought the land at the General Land Office in Little Rock exactly one year before Uriah's purchases.[2] It is highly probable that Martin and Uriah Jones were acquainted in Tennessee before Jones's move to Arkansas. Before going into Uriah's responsibilities for Martin, it is important to get some sense of who they were and the lay of the land they were attaching their fortunes to.

Uriah, born in Virginia in 1806, and Sarah Henderson, born in Illinois, were married in 1832 in Davidson County, Tennessee. The 1840 census places them there with two children under the age of five and lists ownership of four slaves engaged in agriculture. They seem to have come to Arkansas in 1841 because, according to the 1850 census, they had twins born in Arkansas in 1842. According to Uriah's land patent he had located the land he was buying—not an easy task in that dense wilderness for which there had not been township maps before 1846. Until about 1980, when the family gave it to the new Desha County Museum in Dumas, the big brass compass he was said to have used was in the bottom drawer of an old mahogany chest of drawers that had belonged to him. There was also in the house a leather-bound book, published in 1838, *The Revised Acts of Arkansas,* with the words "County Surveyor" still barely discernible on the cover. One wonders whether he had borrowed this book to help him mark his land or whether he worked for the surveyor.

The place they came to was flat, swampy, and dangerous but potentially rich. Desha County, one county removed from the southeast corner of Arkansas, is bordered on the east by the Mississippi River and on the north by the Arkansas and includes the mouth of the White. As if these rivers were not enough, the county is crossed by numerous lesser streams like Bayou Bartholomew and Cypress Creek as well as even smaller ones like Oak Log and Red Fork bayous. The piece of land that Uriah Jones claimed had, as well, several distinctive local water features like Murlatt Bayou and a small lake that had likely been an arm of the Arkansas River at one time. All of the streams have been depositing alluvial soil for thousands of years. This is the heart of the Delta; there is no richer soil in the world. But in the 1840s, when this story begins, this rich soil was so protected from humans by nature that it is a wonder a single field was ever cleared. For an idea of the importance of water in this area, see the map, figure 2. It should be remembered that the running streams and standing bodies of water like lakes and swamps were surrounded with boggy wetlands that provided rich breeding grounds for insects and reptiles. As for flatness, in this county there is a range in altitude of only 35 feet between the highest point near Knowlton Blue Hole in the northeastern part at 160 feet above sea level to the lowest point of 125 feet above sea level near Clay Bayou on the southern boundary.

The story of this farm over the years is also a story about change—unimaginable, unbelievable change—first the transformation of dense swamps and forests into fields, slowly, haltingly, by fits and starts, as small patches were hacked out of the woods and worked by slaves and then by their sharecropping descendants. And then eventually, the small fields were put together into big ones as the trees disappeared, slowly at first because it was difficult to cut them, huge as they were, and then rapidly as the saws improved, until they were all gone—as gone as the people who had cleared the fields and worked them, the axes and hoes and cotton sacks they had used, the plows they guided, and the mules and oxen that pulled them. The only workers who remain now are the few tractor drivers on a landscape almost bare of wild foliage that has been replaced by immense, immaculate, irrigated gardens of cotton, soybeans, wheat, and rice alongside large ponds teeming with domestic catfish, as carefully nurtured as goldfish in a bowl.

When considering change in the part of the world we are discussing here, it is good to remember that farm houses, villages, and even towns can disappear without trace in a very few years because most buildings are built of wood. In Europe, the skeletons of villages unoccupied for years are still there in roofless stone buildings and cobbled streets. By contrast, in the Delta within a few months after a house goes vacant, nature begins retaking its space: weeds eight feet tall fill the yard, vines grow over the house, saplings come up through the porch floor, the roof collapses, and then the whole thing falls down and rots or is eaten by termites. Saplings in the yard become trees and make woods again unless the place gets cleared and planted as part of the field that surrounded it to start with. In a few years, every single trace of human habitation can be erased. The thriving communities and towns in the vicinity of this farm in the nineteenth century—like Napoleon, Montgomery's Point, Arkansas Post, Red Fork, Medford, Cypress Bend, Arkansas City, and Watson—disappeared this way, wholly or partially, in the twentieth century. There are still remnants of Watson and Arkansas City, but the others have either fallen into the Mississippi River or been plowed under. The most spectacular disappearance of all was that of Napoleon, the early county seat of Desha County that had crumbled into the Mississippi except for a few bricks and tombstones by 1872. However, since the Jones family has managed to retain the home place, there is a record of the succession of houses we have lived in over the years.

To comprehend the enormous change I am talking about, it is helpful to listen to the people who saw this country in its wildness, for considering the struggle it took to hang on to this land, much less make a living on it, one wonders what reason to hope there was, in the beginning, for some reward worth enduring the trials that went with taming the territory. Why did people come and why did they stay in this formidable swampland with its endemic diseases like malaria, diphtheria, cholera, and typhoid fever as well as its mosquitoes, ticks, flies, poisonous snakes, panthers, bobcats, bears, and wolves, not to mention the sheer hard work of taming a wilderness? And worst of all perhaps, there was always the mind-numbing boredom in isolated houses separated from others by roads impassable for periods of time to any transportation other than horseback. Without some promise of reward, these people would have had to be insane to leave any remotely decent life they might have had in the East to come looking for a better one here. While contemporary witnesses often seem unsparing in their criticism of the drawbacks, they also provide insight into the reasons people saw fit to come.

We are fortunate to have some eyewitness accounts of the region to fill in our vision of the place that the Jones family came to. The botanist Thomas Nuttall, who visited the area in 1819, the year Arkansas became a territory, described the difficulty of traveling through what sounds like a jungle complete with parrots around Arkansas Post, the oldest settlement west of the Mississippi River and at that time the only place approaching the size of a town for many miles around. The tracts of land that Uriah registered in 1849 were about three miles south of it, across the river in Desha County, which had been formed in 1838. Nuttall described the settlement and its surroundings this way:

> ... The town, or rather settlement of the Post of Arkansas, was somewhat dispersed over a prairie, nearly as elevated as that of the Chicasaw Bluffs, and containing in all between 30 and 40 houses. The merchants, then transacting nearly all the business of the Arkansa and White river, were Messrs. Braham and Drope, Mr. Lewis, and monsieur Notrebe, who kept well-assorted stores of merchandize, supplied chiefly from New Orleans, with the exception of some heavy articles of domestic manufacture obtained from Pittsburgh. Mr. Drope, to whom I was also introduced by letter, received me with politeness, and I could not but now for awhile consider myself as once more introduced into the circle of civilization. ... The cotton produced in this neighborhood, of a quality no way inferior to that of Red river, obtained this year from six to six

and a half dollars per cwt. in the seed, and there were now two gins established for its preparation, though, like everything else, in this infant settlement of the poor and improvident, but little attention beyond that of absolute necessity, was as yet paid to any branch of agriculture. Nature has here done so much, and man so little, that we are yet totally unable to appreciate the value and resources of the soil. Amongst other kinds of grain, rice has been tried on a small scale, and found to answer every expectation. The price of this grain, brought from New Orleans, was no less than 25 to 37½ cents per lb. By retail. Under the influence of a climate mild as the south of Europe, and soil equal to that of Kentucky, wealth will ere long flow, no doubt, to the banks of the Arkansa.[3]

It was the promise of that soil, of course, that encouraged sane people to pack up their belongings and head for it, in spite of the dangers and drawbacks. In fact, enough promise was there for land speculators to be already hard at work when Nuttall made his visit. He reports that one man, a Mr. Winters, owned a million acres.

Within a few years of Nuttall's visit, an entrepreneur named Ben Montgomery opened a trading post and casino at the mouth of the White River to catch the trade going up the Arkansas River before it reached Arkansas Post. The lower reaches of the Arkansas, not being navigable because of current and snags, required large boats coming down or up the Mississippi to unload passengers and cargo destined for the upper Arkansas at Montgomery's Point, where they were transferred to smaller craft that could travel up the White for a few miles and then through a bayou called the "White River Cut-off" to the Arkansas. In the winter of 1838, Cassandra Sawyer Lockwood, a missionary on her way to Dwight Mission in the Cherokee Nation who was stuck at Montgomery's Point for twenty-one days while waiting for a passage, found ample time to observe her surroundings and write reports to the friends she had left behind at the Ipswich Female Seminary in Ipswich, Connecticut. Montgomery's Point was notorious for the gambling that went on there, and Ms. Sawyer was appropriately scandalized by life in the inn itself, which was probably normal for the frontier. Here is her account:

Saugus, January 18, 1838

Respected Young Ladies:

Having passed down the Mississippi to the mouth of the White river, we were informed, one rainy Saturday evening, that we had come to the place of our landing. Here, all the passengers who were going up the Arkansaw were obliged to go on shore, while the "Ohioan" proceeded on her way to New Orleans. The bank of the river at this place we found very steep & clayey, consequently quite difficult of ascent. While ascending, my husband lost his overshoes & was not able to find them. I received the assistance of a Virginian of almost giant strength & was thus enabled to reach the top. This place of landing is called Montgomery's Point & is known to be the greatest sink of iniquity on all the shore[s] of the Mississippi. But this is the only place where travelers can stop who leave the Miss. to go up the Arkansaw. Here is but one family & no other inhabitants are to be found for many miles in either direction. The landlord is a slaveholder and lives in a two-story log house, which is surrounded by numerous little cabins, occupied by his servants. When we arrived, we found nearly 100 persons waiting for a passage up the river, which was so low that no boat could ascend. The landlady was from home & the care of the family was committed to the servants. The next morning was the holy Sabbath but, apparently not remembered in a suitable manner by even one of all our numerous company. The day was regarded only as a holiday. We were summoned to breakfast at 10 o'clock & I asked the servant if this was their usual breakfast hour, to which she replied, "O no, Ma'am; we had to kill a hog this morning before we could get it ready." The wretchedness of our accommodations can be better conceived than described: (& yet the expense of each individual was one dollar per day) as, for instance, they boiled the milk for coffee in an iron kettle placed over a fire out of doors. A swine, in passing along would upset the kettle & then rubbing his nose in it & drinking all that he could, would go away, while the kettle, without being washed, was replaced & more milk poured into it—all went on again as though nothing had happened. . . . but nature's gifts were strikingly rich and beautiful. In one direction from the house, and near to it, was a thin forest & hundreds of beautiful parroquets were daily seen flying from tree to tree. They resemble the parrot so perfectly that it is very difficult to trace any distinction between them. A parroquet, however has never been taught to imitate the human voice. In view of the natural scenery of this place & the moral degradation of its inhabitants, we may appropriately adopt the descriptive language of the poet, "Where every prospect pleases/ And only man is vile."[4]

It is possible that Uriah Jones and his family, like many others, went overland to Memphis, boarded a boat there, and disembarked at Montgomery's Point. It is certain that they would have gone as far as possible by water because of the wretched condition of the trails and traces that served as roads. This letter from George C. Camp to his sister in South Carolina describes the difficulties of getting past the rivers and swamps into farming country. Camp was a teacher with aspirations to become a farmer, and his enthusiasm for his new home and situation are encouraging.

Desha Cty, Ark.
1st April 1851

. . . I came over last October to look at the country and was so well pleased with its appearance that I went back and immediately commenced making arrangements to move, which occupied my time until Christmas or until the 15th December the day on which I bid adieu to my friends in Miss. On the 17 I took a boat at Memphis and came down to Gaines landing 10 miles above a little town called Columbia, occupying one day & night, which cost me 25 dollars though at Memphis we lost a horse worth 60 dollars by falling overboard. We started through the bottom next morning and found it nearly knee deep in mud an[d] water. Our women having to wade, the second day we had traveled twelve miles, and there my wife and sister in law were taken sick from cold and exposure and lay there two weeks, the nearest physicians 25 miles, we looking for them to die hourly, if you ever saw a man in trouble twas I. The Dr came and stayed 2 days and they finally recovered. So far at least as to be able to be hauled out to where we have settled, which is 40 miles west of Gaines landing near Bayou Bartholomew in a beautiful level country of rich land. We settled in the woods, having to take my sick women into a school house until I got a cabin up. I met with the good luck to rent 15 acres of land, 10 of which I intend to plant in cotton and they do say that with a good stand and a good season we may look for a bale to the acre. . . . My children are all fine [and] healthy. Bill Adams is 5 years old and is a fine fellow. Martha Ann is 3 ? and as fat as a pig. George Lewis 8 months & beginning to walk, etc. Our country abounds with deer and turkies, the deer run in sight of the house every day in gangs—I have killed some we have had venison all the time. The wolves and panthers enliven our nights with their serenades. Our creek bottoms are one unbroken cane brake. I am teaching school. I have the best school ever got up in this portion of the country.[5]

As for what the swamp looked like that the Camp family waded through, we must imagine trees of a size that simply do not exist any more. Accustomed as they were to big trees everywhere, the early visitors did not make much of them in their accounts. Both virgin timber and second growth trees were gone, for the most part, from Red Fork Township by 1927, but Eugene Dobson, who moved to Watson as a six-year-old child in 1910, recalled the size of trees still being cut within his memory. In an interview with Mrs. B. R. McGowan for the Desha County Historical Society in 1974 he told of a cypress tree left to rot on the ground because it was too big for the mill. He estimated that it was ten feet in diameter! In addition to the ubiquitous cypress, there were also various kinds of hardwood trees including ash, walnut, pecan, hickory, and locust; different species of oak; cottonwood and willow of various types; and over all, thick, heavy vines that led Nuttall to describe the swamp he waded through to reach Arkansas Post as "a horrible morass." The cypresses, of course, would have been standing in water, surrounded by cypress knees, protuberances from the roots that grow up around the trunk that, for large trees, might reach six or eight feet.

Instead of disembarking at Montgomery's Point or Gaines' Landing, Uriah and family may have landed at Napoleon, situated on the Mississippi at the juncture with the Arkansas, the county seat of

Desha County from 1838 until 1874 when it crumbled into the river as a result of erosion caused by a cut-off ditch dug by Federal troops in 1863 to flush bandits sympathetic to the Confederacy out of the surrounding swamps. It was just a few miles from the Jones farm and, in its heyday between 1850 and 1863, was an important river town, varying in reputation from having the wild lawlessness and squalor of a frontier town to being a local cultural center, surrounded by graceful plantation homes. According to Capt. James Thompson, who visited Napoleon frequently while operating steamboats on the Mississippi and Arkansas, it was a thriving place with a population of about seven thousand, a United States Bank, a federal marine hospital (after 1854), several two-story brick stores, a number of old homes, and the situation of branch operations of several Memphis merchants for whom Thompson's boats unloaded tons and tons of freight. He remembered years later that "the place was filled with culture and refinement." In addition to providing for the needs of local customers, it served as the staging area for freight bound up the Arkansas, with commercial houses in Memphis and New Orleans keeping wharf boats there to insure rapid unloading of their goods.[6]

An entirely different impression was conveyed by Peter Daniel, an associate justice of the United States Supreme Court, who was stuck in Napoleon for an overnight layover, waiting for a boat going up the Arkansas River to Little Rock. This is what he wrote to his daughter, Elizabeth Randolph Daniel:

> Napoleon—Mouth of the Arkansas River,
> April 17th, 1851—5 p.m.

> Dear Daughter, I reached this most wretched of places at twelve o'clock today ... and will not leave this place again until tomorrow evening. This miserable place consists of a few slightly built wooden houses, hastily erected no doubt under some scheme of speculation, and which are tumbling down without ever having been finished—and those which are standing, are some of them without doors or windows. To give an idea of the condition of things, I will state that the best hotel in the place is an old dismantled Steam Boat ... In one of the staterooms of this old Boat I have my chamber about six feet by four; and in what is called the social hall, or more properly the thoroughfare, I am

now writing serenaded by muschetos[*sic*], who are not deterred
from their attack by the motion of my fingers, on which they
constantly fasten; whilst out of doors, they are joined by what
in this region is called the Buffalo Gnat; an insect so fierce & so
insatiate, that it kills horses & mules bleeding them to death. I
devotedly love the south, but I could not live in that portion of
it which is subjected to these evils. But in despite of them, the
Yankees flock hither as numerously almost as the insects & flour-
ish & fatten amongst them. . . .

. . . The mail boat has arrived so in a few hours I shall leave
this "delectable" City of Napoleon without the exception of
some cold from unavoidable exposure—and the hours of filth
in every shape & degree, I am well—with love to all at home
your affectionate father—P. V. Daniel.[7]

In that same month, a young Irishman named James Kerr moved
to Napoleon and subsequently wrote his uncle James Graham in
County Antrim, Ireland, the following report about the new country. It tells a great deal more about the day-to-day quality of life in
the region than Justice Daniel's letter. It is interesting that Kerr's ambi-
tion is to own a store in a river town, but not this one.

May 25th, 1851

Dear Uncle, . . . I came to this place, "Napoleon," in the
beginning of April. I was not doing well at New Orleans and
got an offer of better wages to come here. It is a small village,
situated at the mouth of the Arkansas river, 640 miles above New
Orleans. A merchant of N. O. and one of this state established a
house here, to do a general business, grocery, Dry goods, etc., &
also for the purpose of re-shipping goods left here by Cincinnati
& New Orleans boats intended for the interior of this state. The
concern is a new one, but is doing pretty well. I keep the Books
& attend things in general. I get $50 per month & found in
board, etc., which is equal to $80 in New Orleans without board,
which is considered good wages there. There are other advantages, however, which make the situation worth more, that is by
forming acquaintance & learning something of the country. I
probably can, before long, get into business on my own account.
A new country presents a much better prospect for that than a

city or an old country. I wish I had come here—to this state rather—instead of going to Pennsylvania & killing myself teaching school for nearly nothing & studying what has been of no pecuniary advantage to me. Why, the best wages in Pennsylvania for teaching was $20, in one or two places $25 without board. The other day, a planter across the river [Mississippi] offered me $250 for 10 months to teach his family about 4 children, & give board, washing etc. besides. That would be $25 per month clear. Now James could get that if he was here now. . . . I would advise him to come out here. I can get him plenty of situations to teach—the schools will be small, perhaps only a family or two & he can do it well. People are anxious to get teachers, many, I might say most of the Planters have to send their children from home 4 or 500 miles & they would much rather employ a teacher at home. . . . This is a fine healthy state, when you get back from the Mississippi. There are many flourishing towns in it & it is settling fast. I expect to settle in some healthy little town on the Arkansas river, bye and bye, & have a share in a store. I have one or two places in view where a store will do well, & when I have about $2,000 capital, I can commence for myself. I do wish I had come to Arkansas 10 years ago.

This place "Napoleon" is but very small, containing about 100 inhabitants. It is not a pleasant place to live. The Mississippi overflows it every year, sometimes twice; this renders it unhealthy. They are going to make a "levee" [embankment] this year to keep out the water. It has good facilities for trade & many say that in 10 years, it will be a large place. The *people* of the place are not like those of the North. In fact, the Southern Americans are different from the Northern a great deal. They are far inferior in intelligence & morality. They have not the same steady, sober, peaceable, persevering & enterprising character possessed by their Northern brethren. Many of them are ignorant [unable to read], rude, filthy in their habits & intemperate. Those of this town particularly so, especially as to filth & intemperance. Drinking is their principal, I might say their only enjoyment. . . . This county consumes a vast quantity of "liquor" & it presents a greater amount of mortality, taken from the statistics of the state, than any other county in it.

. . . This part of the United States is almost exclusively a cotton growing country & it is considered the best for that article of any other in the country. Farming is done altogether by negroes; Planters owning from 10 to 100 of these. The land is very rich and planters have done well the last 2 or 3 years, cotton having been high for three seasons. An acre produces, if I remember right, about 500 pounds cotton, which sells for about $50—I believe they raise sometimes 800 pounds. [8]

But the most famous observer of life in Napoleon was undoubtedly Mark Twain, who is thought to have used it as a model for the town in the shameful episode in *Adventures of Huckleberry Finn* where Huck witnesses the murder of Boggs, the harmless town drunk, by the pitiless, arrogant Colonel Sherburn for insults delivered under the influence of alcohol. Twain returns to it again in *Life on the Mississippi* in a fanciful tale that ends with his narrator's attempt to stop there again on a trip down the river many years later only to find the town gone.

> Yes, it was an astonishing thing to see the Mississippi rolling between unpeopled shores and straight over the spot where I used to see a good big self-complaisant town twenty years ago. Town that was county seat of a great and important county; town with a big United States Marine Hospital; town of innumerable fights—an inquest every day; town where I had used to know the prettiest girl, and the most accomplished in the whole Mississippi Valley; town where we were handed the first printed news of the Pennsylvania's mournful disaster a quarter of a century ago; a town no more—swallowed up, vanished, gone to feed the fishes; nothing left but a fragment of a shanty and a crumbling brick chimney.[9]

Sir Henry Morton Stanley, who later attained fame by finding Dr. Livingstone in Africa, arrived in Cypress Bend, a Desha County community on the Mississippi, in November 1860 to spend a few months clerking in a store. Perhaps it was his perception as an Englishman well acquainted with a rigid class system that gave him a different view of the local social structure from those of his fellow clerks. He later wrote this account of his experience at Cypress Bend in his autobiography:

[B]y this time I had become sufficiently acquainted with the tone of the planter community to be able to do very well, with a few instructions from Mr. Altshul. I had learned that in the fat cypress lands there was a humanity which was very different from that complaisant kind dwelling in cities. It had been drawn from many States, especially from the South. The Douglasses were from Virginia, the Crawfords from "Old Georgia," the Joneses and Smiths from Tennessee, the Gorees from Alabama. The poorer sort were from the Carolinas, Mississippi, Missouri, and Tennessee, the professional men and white employers from a wider area—which included Europe. Several of the richer men owned domains of from six to ten square miles. . . . Though genially sociable to each other, to landless people like myself they conducted themselves as though they were under no obligations. . . . their bearing seemed to say that they yielded to us every privilege belonging to free whites, but reserved to themselves the right to behave as they deemed fitting to their state, and of airing any peculiarity unquestioned, and unremarked by the commonalty. They were as exclusive as the proud county families of Wales. . . . My proud fellow clerks were disposed to think it was the dread of the pistol which made them so guarded in speech and action, but I thought that it was the fear of compromising the personal dignity by a disgraceful squabble with men untaught in the forms of good society. . . . It is wonderful what trivial causes were sufficient to irritate them. A little preoccupation in one's own personal affairs, a monosyllabic word, a look of doubt, or a hesitating answer, made them flare up hotly. The true reason for this excessive sensitiveness was that they had lived too much within their own fences, and the taciturnity engendered by exclusiveness had affected their habits. However amiable they might originally have been, their isolation had promoted the growth of egotism and self-importance.[10]

Such was the neighborhood that the Jones family settled into. Arkansas Post, Napoleon, Gaines' Landing, and Cypress Bend were all within a few hours ride by horseback of the farm.

The spot that Uriah Jones chose for his house was at the top of a rise called Pea Ridge. A surveyor's map made in 1840 shows a small lake with the remnant of a stream still visible at its lower edge. This lake, probably an arm of the Arkansas River some time in the distant past, had dwindled by 1930 to a swamp that went dry every summer except for a small hole where any aquatic life that could took refuge until the fall rains. The house and barns were built on the top of a worn-down bluff that provided a natural run-off to keep them dry during periods of high water. The houses later built by his son Joseph and his grandson Boss were situated on the same bluff, about a quarter of a mile north of Uriah's spot. The Great Flood of 1927 was the exception in the matter of flooding, and the houses must have been solidly built to withstand the force of that current. But that is a story for two generations on.

CHAPTER 2

The Uriah Generation

1849–1872

One story, told me in passing by my father, had it that Uriah was a mule trader when he came to Arkansas in 1841, and as selling mules on the frontier was lucrative and as he did come to Arkansas from Davidson County, Tennessee, the center of the mule-trading world, it may be true. The 1840 census for Davidson County lists him as owning four slaves, so he probably did not come to the frontier penniless. But whatever his prospects on arrival, by 1850 he was overseer of a plantation in Red Fork Township, Desha County, obviously belonging to an absent owner, as Uriah Jones is shown in the 1850 census to be in charge, with the production and slaves listed in his name. Family legend has it that this was the plantation now known as the "Haywire Farm," which adjoins the Jones family farm on the north. The Haywire Farm is notorious for its difficulties, many of which stem from its proximity to the Arkansas River, and my father liked to say that his grandfather had been the first to meet his match on it. Beautiful to look at and a temptation to anyone with the inclination to farm and enough credit to buy it, this plantation has, in fact, through the years driven many of its owners into bankruptcy.

At the time, it belonged to George W. Martin, who is listed in

Desha County with late-nineteenth-century towns and water features.

the 1850 Free Population Census in Davidson County, Tennessee, as
"Sec., Insurance Office," with property valued at $30,000. According
to the slave schedule, Martin owned 17 slaves in Tennessee. He
bought 779.7 acres from the United States government at the Land
Office at Little Rock on November 1, 1848, ten months before
Jones's first purchase was recorded.[1] Martin died in 1853, leaving the
Arkansas property to his wife Narcissa and his son-in-law Joseph

Branch. Known as the Martin-Branch Plantation in 1860 (presumably when Uriah was no longer associated with it), it had 183 slaves and 3,550 acres listed in the census. It is likely that George W. Martin and Uriah Jones were clearing and working their land before their purchases were finalized with the government, as Jones assessed his 200 acres in 1848 at $1,000, a year before he got title to it, according to the dates on his deeds.

In the 1850 census Uriah and his family are listed in the free population schedule for Red Fork Township as Urias [*sic*] Jones, "Overseer," age 46; wife Sarah, age 28; son Joseph, age 11; daughters Amanda and Elizabeth, ages 7; daughter Adalade, age 4; and daughter Frances, age two.[2] Joseph, of course, was born in Tennessee and his younger siblings in Arkansas. Of these, Amanda, Elizabeth, and Adalade apparently died before the 1860 census. A "Fannie V. Jones" who may have been Joseph's sister Frances, also absent from the 1860 census, is listed in the family Bible as being born in 1849 and dying in 1898 as "Fannie V. Coopwood." (Ages listed in the census rolls are not always reliable; Uriah was actually born in 1808, according to the records in the family Bible, and Joseph in November 1837, making them 42 and 13, respectively, in 1850.) Uriah's real estate was valued at $1,000 because by 1850 he had the 200 acres of land of his own that became the family farm.

According to the agriculture schedule of the 1850 census, where he is listed as "farmer," the plantation he was overseeing was a thriving establishment with a total of 3,500 acres of which 600 were "improved" and 2,900 "unimproved." Its cash value was $2,300 (more likely $23,000) and the value of implements $800. For livestock there were 1 horse, 20 mules, 15 milch cows, 11 working oxen, 25 other cattle, 6 sheep, and 100 swine, for a total value of $2,000. Its production for 1849 was 4,000 bushels of corn, 400 400-pound bales of ginned cotton, and 20 tons of hay. Animals sold for slaughter brought $100.[3]

The slave schedule lists 61 slaves, the third largest number of slaves on a plantation in Desha County at that time after the numbers owned by William P. Warfield and John M. Taylor.

If Uriah was indeed a mule skinner when he came in 1841, he

had risen to a position of responsibility in a relatively short time, a rise
that is perhaps evidence for the opportunity that existed for able men
on this frontier. The overseer of a plantation belonging to an absentee owner was the boss. It was his job to oversee the day-to-day operations of the place as well as to clear new land to expand the property.
As for compensation, good overseers were paid well enough to enable
them to set money aside to invest in property of their own. Francis
Terry Leak, an absentee owner of Arkansas property who lived in
Mississippi, noted in his diary the terms under which he employed
George Townsend in 1857:

> I am to pay him wages of $400 pr year, & am to find him bread
> for his family, also 600 lbs flour, 150 lbs sugar, 75 lbs coffee and
> his meat, with the exception of 500 lbs pork which he is to
> furnish & put in the smoke house. I am also to feed his horse.
> He is to bring no stock on the plantation and is to keep but
> one horse.[4]

In 1861, Leak made the following reference to the employment
of James Sergeant for the same position:

> [He] is to be provided with all his bread, including 300 to 400
> lbs flour; 50 lbs sugar, 5 to 10 gallons molasses; a negro boy to
> cut his wood, make his fires, feed his horse & draw a bucket
> of water, night & morning; a negro woman to cook and wash
> for him whenever his wife is sick; and $350 wage.[5]

And this is where the telling of the family story becomes painful,
for the success of clearing this swampland and making it profitable
must have depended on the lash, and Uriah was in charge of the dis-
cipline of men being worked like animals. Let us try to imagine the
difficulty of the work at hand. The trees themselves, some of them
ten or twelve feet in diameter, had gigantic root systems that had to
be cleared for the plow. And the trees were covered with vines and
surrounded with underbrush that had to be removed before the trees
could be dealt with. All this had to be done with hand tools in a
humid climate with frequent rainfall and seemingly bottomless mud.
(A man who cleared land adjacent to this farm in about 1936 told me
in an interview a few years ago that in order to do it he worked sunup

to sundown, rain or shine. He had two sets of denim work clothes that were sometimes never dry for days at a time. His wife washed his muddy shirt and pants at night, and they would still not be dry when he put them on a day later. He said the only thing that kept the work from killing him was the incentive of becoming a landowner.[6]) It was a different matter for the slaves who had been ripped out of whatever state of comfort they had enjoyed in the east and driven to this godforsaken place of interminable work and disease. Their only incentive must have been to stay alive.

And the clearing had to be done as quickly as possible. Donald McNeilly, in his masterful study *The Old South Frontier,* describes the way the new landowners went about clearing their land in order to have at least a semblance of a crop the first year. The aim was for the pioneering party to arrive in winter or early spring, set up camp and first cut timber suitable for rails, then cut and burn undergrowth, then cut and stockpile wood for enough fuel for several seasons, then "deaden" the large trees by cutting a ring around each tree through the bark hoping they would fall in a high wind. After a few months, when trees and brush were dry enough, there would be a "grand burning" after which the field would be enclosed with rails and planted. Planters could count on the first year's crop to pay for the clearing. As early as the next December, the end of the year in which they arrived, cotton would have been pressed and sent to market, and cash would be flowing to buy food and amenities for slaves and masters. In the second year they could count on a bale of cotton or thirty bushels of corn per acre.[7]

The term "overseer" was a bad word for good reason then and is so to this day; presumably, nobody would want to be an overseer who could be a "planter," and within a few years, Uriah Jones had added substantially to his property and status and was on his way to being a "planter" himself.

In 1858 he assessed 600 acres of land valued at $2,520, 8 slaves between the ages of 5 and 60 valued at $2,600, 1 carriage worth $70, 5 horses and mules worth $375, 13 cows worth $140, and jewelry worth $140, on which he paid a total state tax of $11.30 and a county tax of $17.32.[8] In the 1860 census he styled himself "planter" for the census taker, as did his 23-year-old son Joseph, and had an overseer of his own living in his household. The 1860 Arkansas Free Population Census lists the following for household #162: Uriah Jones, age 52, planter; Sarah Jones, housekeeper; Joseph, age 23, planter; Adeline, age 14; Frances, age 11; A. J. Bridges, age 34, overseer; Ann (Bridges), age 27, housekeeper; and Edward (Bridges), age 8.[9]

According to the agriculture schedule, the Jones family now owned 440 acres of which 100 were "improved" and 340 were not. The cash value of the farm was $15,000, value of implements $50. There were 10 horses, 1 mule, 12 milch cows, 4 oxen, 18 other cows, and 50 swine, worth a total of $1,800. In 1859 the farm produced 800 bushels of corn, thirty-five 400-pound bales of cotton, 100 bushels of peas and beans, 20 bushels of sweet potatoes, and 100 pounds of butter. (There is nothing in the records to account for his assessing 600 acres in 1858 and claiming only 440 on the 1860 census—the former was probably a mistake, corrected by his 1861 assessment of 440 acres.)

The 1860 slave schedule lists Uriah Jones with the ownership of 8 slaves, only 3 of whom were over the age of 16, certainly not enough labor to produce the crops listed. However, Joseph, who is also listed as a "planter" and member of his father's household, assessed 8 slaves of his own for tax purposes, bringing the number of adult workers to 12. Their joint assessments for 1861 help clarify the picture given by the census entries. Uriah assessed 440 acres of land (N1/2 13 9S 3W, 320 acres; N1/2 SE13 9S 3W, 80 acres; and NE SW13 9S 3W, 40 acres) valued at $5,280. He assessed 4 slaves valued at $2,800, 1 carriage at $75, 7 horses at $490, 16 cows at $128, and jewelry at $125. The total value of his property was $8,898 on which he owed taxes of $22.24 to Desha County and $29.66 to the state of Arkansas. Joseph assessed no land, but he had 8 slaves valued at $6,400, 1 horse worth $100, 4 mules worth $500, and 2 cows worth $40, for a total of $7,040 in taxable property on which he owed $18.60 to the federal government and $23.46 to the state.[10]

No daguerreotypes of Uriah and Sarah remain, but there is a brief description of Uriah on the amnesty list, found in the Desha County Courthouse in Arkansas City in 1986. (In 1865, President Andrew Johnson issued a proclamation granting a pardon that restored United

States citizenship to all citizens of the Confederate States on condition of their taking an oath of loyalty to the United States. The exceptions to this general amnesty were former officers of the Confederate Army and those owning more than $20,000 worth of taxable property, who could also be pardoned under proper petition.) Uriah and Joseph signed this oath of loyalty before Provost Marshal J. D. Loyd at Memphis, Tennessee, on July 2, 1865. This is his entry: "Uriah Jones, born in Virginia, age 58, 5 feet ten inches tall, grey hair and light eyes, a farmer."[11] We lack also any pictures of the house they lived in—it was no longer standing within the memory of anyone still alive, although the spot where it had stood was pointed out to us as children. More than likely their first house was made of logs with a dogtrot and stick chimneys, almost certainly with the kitchen situated in another structure.

The only pieces of furniture left that are definitely associated with the first generation of this family in Arkansas are a big chest of drawers and a four-poster bed that originally had a tester to hold up a mosquito bar. Joseph and his siblings were born in it as were his children—including my father Grover Cleveland and his children, including me. Joseph's middle initial "H" (for Hubbard) is cut in one post at the eye level of a small child.

Uriah was a reader, as evidenced by the "family library" worth $15 that he was allowed to keep when he declared bankruptcy in 1868, as did many others in the area. The books were still there in 1942 when my mother gave them, with all the other books in the house, to the Watson school to replace those lost in a schoolhouse fire. They had been saved from the 1927 Flood and carefully kept with those added by Joseph and others "so we would not grow up like savages with nothing to read," to quote Mother. (She ironed the pages after the flood.) When the schoolhouse burned, she said she could not bear the thought of a school without books and that we could read them there with the other children.

The cotton business was booming in Desha County in 1860. In the ten years between the 1850 and 1860 censuses the number of improved acres of land had increased from 9,207 to 42,264 with the number of ginned bales rising from 2,672 to 12,261. The white population grew from 1,742 to 2,655 and the slave population from 1,169 to 3,784.[12] So the world must have looked rosy to the Jones family in 1860, although even in their isolation they would have been aware of the storm clouds gathering. In 1865, when the dust settled after Appomattox, Uriah Jones was on what looked like the road to ruin, or at least a path toward drastically altered expectations. The man who had been on the rise in 1860 had become a man desperately treading water—a legacy of desperation he passed down to his son Joseph who in turn passed it to his son Grover Cleveland, "Boss."

Being on the losing side of the war at the end of hostilities was made worse, of course, by the difficulties endured in surviving it. For example, the closest pitched battle, for the Post of Arkansas on January 11, 1863, took place some five or six miles away, across the Arkansas River on the bank of the Mississippi. But this short episode involved, all told, some 35,000 troops who had to be fed, and one suspects the major portion of their rations was foraged from the surrounding countryside. Even in the absence of formal battles, however, the farm's proximity to the river guaranteed attention by patrols from both armies as well as guerillas who roamed the entire region, taking whatever they needed or fancied. Witness to the prevalence of Confederate-sympathizing guerillas in Desha County is the fact that there were so many of them in the swamps on the peninsula near where Napoleon was situated at the mouth of the Arkansas that the Federal army cut a ditch across it to drown them out and so hastened the erosion that would slide the entire town into the Mississippi River by 1872. The tales of hardship the war caused were still being told around the house eighty-five years later. One concerned a neighbor woman who saw a patrol approaching the front gate of her yard and ran to the smokehouse to try to hide as much meat as she could. She grabbed a ham, ran out the door with it, and seeing that she would be caught, pretended to fall down, sitting on the ham concealed under her skirts until the men left, taking everything else from the smokehouse with them. This was, of course, said to be a Yankee patrol. (Who else would have left that poor woman sitting on the ground without offering to help her up!) It might as easily have been others: Confederate soldiers, partisans, or just plain bandits. My brother-in-law's grandfather answered a knock on the gate one night and was never seen again. Nobody knew who the men were who took him, or why.

There was a large cannonball in our yard when I was a child. Nobody could account for its origin except to say that it was left over from the war. My mother painted it silver and put it in a flower bed as a point of interest where it served to remind us of our romantic past, as the Civil War had come to be thought of by that time. But it was certainly not romantic while it was going on. People almost starved to death in the winters; the war's interference with river traffic kept the family from getting the goods they were accustomed to acquiring from Memphis and from sending the things they usually sold for cash. Cotton was stolen by thieves of both Confederate and Union sympathies.

But the hardship of survival was a mere prelude to the monumental problems Uriah Jones had to face when the conflict was over. The most important financial consideration, of course, was the loss of his hold on his labor force. Even assuming that family legend is correct and the freed slaves remained on the place, the working relationship was changed forever. And although the different terms that had to be negotiated with the freedmen were perhaps in his favor, they were undoubtedly less profitable.

There is no record of Uriah's contract with his laborers during Reconstruction; however, a letter from the superintendent of the Freedmen's Bureau in Monticello to B. W. Thomas in Desha County, whose situation must have been analogous to Uriah's, dated November 27, 1866, lists terms contracted between Mr. Thomas and his workers on January 5, 1866:

> Genie Blankenship, Age 40, $10 per month and good clothing
> Aggie Blankenship, Age 40, $10 per month and good clothing
> Charles Martin, Age 37, $10 per month and good clothing
> Margaret Martin, Age 30, $6 per month and good clothing
> Luci Williams, Age 21, $5 per month and good clothing
> William Thomas, Age 12, $5 per month and good clothing
> Starling Jones, Age 63, $80 for the year and good clothes
> Mary A. Jones, Age 35, $80 for the year and good clothes

You also furnish all needful medicines and medical attention and substantial cabins. The hands do good and faithful service under your direction or that of your legal agent and work
from sunup to sundown with reasonable time for noon . [13]

This obligation, in a contract with the federal government at a
time when credit for cash to buy seed and put the crop in was harder
to come by than it had previously been, must have been a terrifying
thing. In addition, a new Draconian tax structure had to be dealt with,
and worse weather conditions for raising cotton could not be imagined than those prevailing from 1866 to 1869. On top of all this, a
drastic fall in the price of cotton in the fall of 1867 made it hardly
worth planting.

Uriah Jones's problems need to be seen in the context of the total
postwar situation in Arkansas, for he was not alone. It was probably
small comfort that most if not all of the farmers in the state were in
much the same boat, as disaster followed disaster in the rest of cot-
ton-dependent Arkansas as well as on the Jones farm. Carl Moneyhon,
in *The Impact of the Civil War and Reconstruction on Arkansas,* paints a
devastating picture of the destructive forces let loose against farmers
in the Delta in 1866. He says that the limited success of the 1865 farming operations and the high price of cotton led to optimism about
prospects for the 1866 crop that were dashed by weather and a plague
of army worms. However, the price of thirty-seven cents a pound was
enough to spark enthusiasm for planting in the spring of 1867; at this
price, one good crop of cotton could pay off debts and make a profit.
(In 1860 the average price had been eleven cents a pound.) But once
again the weather did not cooperate, and the result was a disastrously
short crop. To make things worse, the price fell to seventeen or eighteen cents a pound by October 1867. This was the beginning of a trend
of hard times that lasted, with occasional relief, until the prosperity
brought by World War II. Moneyhon puts it succinctly:

> Weather conditions continued to be bad, with either late springs,
> flooding, or drought in 1868, 1869, and 1874. Cutworms were
> particularly bad in 1869. Worse, the market for cotton remained
> soft and prices low. For several years after the price collapse of
> 1867, market prices ranged between 12 and 18 cents per pound,

although individual farmers could seldom count on those prices, since they usually dealt with local merchants paying prices 25 percent less than at market. In 1874 cotton hit 11.1 cents a pound, then began a precipitous fall that bottomed with the disastrous price of 5.8 cents a pound in the period from 1894 to 1897.[14]

As for the individual difficulties enumerated above, taxes presented immediate problems for the Jones family at the end of the war. According to the records, in 1866 Uriah Jones fought successfully to avoid paying $66 in levee taxes on his land, at that time comprising 440 acres.[15] But other taxes had to be paid, and the rate was exorbitant by prewar standards. For although Federal victory invalidated Confederate state taxes for the war years, Confederates owed state taxes levied by the Republican government after 1864 as well as the 1861 United States direct tax. State taxes amounted to a combined rate of 3 percent on each $100 worth of property (compared to a rate of .5 percent before the war), and the 1861 direct tax was .37 percent.[16] Taxation continued to get worse; in 1868, after Arkansas's restoration to the Union, the Republican legislature raised taxes to support the reforms they adopted in education and to finance railroads. The new state tax was three times that imposed by the previous General Assembly, and county taxes were one and a half times higher.[17]

In 1867, Uriah assessed 440 acres worth $13,211, 3 horses at $225, 2 mules worth $200, and 27 cows worth $425, for a total assessed value of $2,170. He was assessed $21.70 for road tax, $4.34 for school tax, $23.70 county tax, and $32.55 for state tax. Joseph apparently had nothing.[18]

According to Moneyhon, hope prevailed over despair at the end of the war in 1865. Older men, women, and children got the crops planted that year as well as they could, and the young men returning from the army fell to as soon as they reached home. But many, including Joseph who by his account did not start walking home from North Carolina until Confederate general Joseph E. Johnston's surrender on May 26, did not get home in time to help with the planting but were there in time for the harvest.

There are no family papers illuminating the day-to-day events of

these years, but the reports of the superintendent of the Freedmen's
Bureau at Napoleon, Capt. J. C. Predmore, are heart rending in their
descriptions of the destitution suffered by both black and white citizens of Desha County, plantation owners as well as former slaves and
landless white people:

June 1, 1867

> The high waters of the Mississippi and Ark. Rivers sub-
> sided about the first of the month and planters commenced
> planting in earnest and on many plantations there was a fine
> stand of cotton by the 20th and 25th but the Rivers are at pres-
> ent rising again very rapidly . . . several large cotton fields are
> under water at this date and the water is rising rapidly—will
> probably reach from two to three feet above its present highth
> which will ruin the prospects for cotton for the present year
> in nearly all the southern portion of this county . . .

June 30, 1867

> A large number of the Freedmen in the eastern and southron
> portions of the county have left the plantations on which they
> contracted by the mutual consent of the Freedmen and planter
> on those plantations which were overflowed until it became too
> late to plant a crop of cotton and in a number of instances from
> the fact that the planters were unable to procure supplies to feed
> their hands during the season. Many plantations have been aban-
> doned entirely and on a number of others only a small portion
> of the land is being cultivated. . . . the future prospects are such
> as to require the serious attention of Government and State offi-
> cials. Even planters owning large tracts of land are unable to
> obtain the necessary supplies to feed their families and labor.
> Nearly all the landowners in this county have encumbrances on
> their land to such an amount as to unable them to get supplies
> on real estate securities and merchants will not advance on the
> present crop with that for security . . . cases of destitution are
> increasing daily . . . .[19]

These terrible conditions naturally took their toll, and according
to family lore, Uriah, seeing disaster looming, decided to sell Joseph
the bulk of his land to try keep it in the family. The transaction took

place on February 7, 1868. He sold it to Joseph for $900, retaining for himself the northeast quarter of S13 T9S R3W, the 160 acres he would be allowed to keep as homestead in bankruptcy.[20] Joseph duly recorded this in his fine leather-bound pocket notebook along with cotton weights for pickers, a remedy for smallpox, his shirt size, and numerous other bits of information he would not want to lose track of.[21] One wonders how much, if any, of the land transferred to Joseph had been cleared.

On October 5, 1868, Uriah Jones was issued a certificate of exempted property from bankruptcy "under the provisions of the 14th Section of the Act of Congress entitled An Act to Establish a Uniform system of Bankruptcy throughout the United States," which had been approved March 2, 1867. This is what he was allowed to keep, according to the creased and yellowed certificate from Aunt Sallie's trunk:

> Necessary household and kitchen furniture not exceeding $500. in value; Other articles and necessaries; Wearing apparel of Bankrupt and his family; Equipments, if any, as a Soldier; Other Property exempted by laws of the United States:

1 Bedstead & Bedding	$20.00
Sideboard	7.00
2 cows $20. 2 yearling colts $10.	30.00
Hogs $25. ox cart $25.	50.00
1 plow $1. Hoes .50 ox 15.	21.5

Property exempted by State laws:
NE1/4 Sec 15 T9 SR2w

160 acres valued at $800.	800.00
2 Bedsteads & Bedding	40.00
Bureau 8. Chairs 10.	18.00
Table & Kitchen Furniture	30.00
Wearing Apparel of Self & Family	50.00
Household stoves	20.00
Family Library	15.00
Cow 10. Plow 1. [Illegible] .50	11.50

The 1870 census shows a smaller household for Uriah Jones. Household #420 lists only Uriah, age 64, farmer; Sarah, age 47, housekeeper; and a black woman named Martha Brown, age 40, housekeeper. (One wonders if this might be the woman Uriah bought on September 10, 1852, according to a deed record: "Received of Uriah Jones Eight hundred dollars for one Negroe woman named Martha age 18 & her child Eliza nine months old which I warrant to be sound both in body and mind and slaves for life . . . Signed William T. Samples."[22]) Presumably Uriah's daughters were either dead or married and gone by this time, although the records are strangely silent about them; we know that Joseph was in Tennessee getting married.

In the same census, Uriah Jones's real estate was valued at $1,600 and his personal property at $1,000. The agriculture schedule gives the following information about the farm: improved land, 60 acres; woodland, 100 acres; value of farm, $1,600; value of implements, $75; wages paid, $100; 2 horses; 3 mules; 2 milch cows; 4 working oxen; 19 other cattle; 14 sheep; 30 swine; value of stock, $800. Produce: 100 bushels of corn, six 450-pound bales of cotton, 50 bushels of peas and beans, 100 bushels of Irish potatoes, and 200 pounds of butter. The estimated value of farm produce was $930.[23]

Something might be said here about the amount of work it took to produce the products listed during Uriah's tenure as manager of this farm, with some speculation about who did it. As for the crops listed in the 1860 census, it may be reasonably assumed that most of the work was done by the slaves, but frequently on farms as small as this one, with 440 acres, the owner worked in the fields as well. James T. Trulock, who arrived in 1848 as master of a much larger establishment in nearby Jefferson County, wrote letters to family back in Georgia and Connecticut describing his work beside his slaves in the fields and in constructing the necessary buildings for the farming operation.[24] Perhaps both Uriah *and* his overseer worked in the fields.

According to statistics compiled by the census bureau, in 1840 it took 438 man-hours to produce a bale of cotton.[25] Probably few technical advances had been made to lighten this load by 1860. So in that year on the Jones farm, at least 15,330 hours were spent in bringing in 35 bales of cotton, weighing 400 pounds each. This meant an average workload of 1,277.5 man-hours for each of the twelve slaves, on the cotton crop alone, if they did all the work. At the New Orleans market price of 11.1¢ per pound, the cash crop for the farm that year would have brought $15,540, less at the gin in Arkansas. But since the farm had to be almost totally self-sufficient, in addition to the labor required to work the cotton, a tremendous effort had to go into the crops that would feed everyone on the place, like corn, peas, beans, potatoes, milk, and butter, with provisions for livestock as well, including a large number of hogs to provide the pork that was the mainstay of their diet. Horses, oxen, poultry, and hogs would have had to be fed grain, although undoubtedly the rest of the livestock would have been allowed to forage in the surrounding woods. There was hay growing on the prairie across the Arkansas River free for anyone with the energy and means to cut it and haul it home.

The fields Uriah worked would have been small and surrounded by forest. For the first several years, they probably plowed around the stumps with the primitive one-row, ox- or mule-drawn plows in use at the time. The weeds and grass would have been controlled by extensive hoeing, and cotton would have been picked into bags dragged behind each picker. Techniques improved only slightly over the next seventy years or so, until the invention of the two-row cultivator and then the tractor. It is impossible to know how many bales he got to the acre. (One of the fields he worked was undoubtedly the one Casey, his great-great-grandson, calls "cemetery field," near the spot where Uriah's house stood and so one of the first fields cleared.)

By 1870, Uriah would have had to rely on sharecroppers or day labor to get his work done, and he probably had to go into the fields himself, his circumstances having been so considerably reduced. In fact, his entire household, including his wife, may well have had to do field work. The only land listed in the 1870 census for the farm is the 160 acres he was allowed to retain in the bankruptcy proceedings. No mention is made of Joseph, who was probably still in Tennessee where he had gone to get married, when the census taker came round.

Uriah was unable to pay all his taxes in 1871, so eighty acres of his land were forfeited to the state, but as it sometimes happened in this family, it was retrieved by a fluke, this time by his son Joseph in 1875. It is interesting that although Joseph was the legal owner of most of the land after he bought it from his father in 1868, Uriah continued to assess it and pay taxes on it until his death.

According to the record in the Jones family Bible, Uriah Jones died on June 27, 1872. Tradition has it that he was buried in the Porter Graveyard near Watson. Most of the members of subsequent generations have been buried in the family cemetery on the farm, a stone's throw from the site of Uriah's house. There is confusion about the date of his wife's demise, for although Sarah is listed in every census through 1870, the *Goodspeed Biographical History of Southern Arkansas* states that she died about 1842, having borne a family of five children: Joseph, another son John who died in 1842, and then three daughters, Addie who died in 1873, Amanda who died in 1878, and Elizabeth who died in 1879. There is no mention of Sarah's birth or death in the family records nor of the daughters', unless Joseph's sister Frances is the Fannie Coopwood listed in the Bible record as dying in 1898.

The quality of life in the Jones household during Uriah's tenure must remain a matter of speculation. We know they were readers with broad interests by the books they left that ranged in subject matter from biography to scientific studies to fiction. They were Presbyterians, but we do not know how deeply their religion was felt. We know nothing about the kind of social life they had. According to the tax records, they had a "pleasure carriage," and Sarah had jewelry. But one wonders where they went in that carriage on the muddy or dusty roads and what were the occasions for her to wear her finery. From the evidence of public records we can reconstruct a semblance of a neighborhood. They were not alone out there in the middle of those swamps and woods. There were as many or more people living in the immediate vicinity of their house in the decade between 1850 and 1860 as there are in 2006. Some, at least, must have had the same ideals and aspirations that the Joneses had. According to the General Land Office Records, in August and November 1849, when Uriah Jones received ownership of lands in sections 12 and 13 of township 9N, so did William Murlatt, Samuel Brackenridge, William Purssell, James Felts, George Martin, and

William Bradford.[26] The only members of this group of landhold-
ers to be listed in the 1850 census are Margaret Murlatt and her
family of eight children, household #174. (Uriah's household was
#173.) So, at the very least, there was another family within a half
mile of the Jones household. The Murlatts left their name on a
little bayou. We do not know whether the Joneses neighbored with
the Murlatts, but it is certain that they did make friends with Calvin
Stroud and his family, who lived a few miles away in section 27,
township 9S, and who received a patent for eighty acres on
December 1, 1849. Calvin Stroud's youngest son, Alfred, eventually
married Uriah's granddaughter and became a character in the Jones
family narrative during Joseph's tenure. And soon, also within three
miles, the Moore, Irby, and Coopwood families settled, and friend-
ships were forged that have lasted to this day.

Joseph
Hubbard
Jones.
Wedding
picture,
1869.
*Author's
collection*.

Mary
Margaret
Brown
Jones.
Wedding
picture,
1869.
*Author's
collection*.

--- CHAPTER 3 ---

The Joseph Generation

1872–1906

W hile our attention has been focused on Uriah and his fortunes, Joseph has been preparing to take center stage. His wedding picture, a daguerreotype taken in October 1869, shows a handsome young man with big ears and deep-set, weary, worried eyes. His left hand, resting on a cane as it is in other pictures of him, is missing its third finger, which he himself had finished amputating after a Minié ball left it hanging by a sliver of skin during the Battle of Atlanta. If ever a bridegroom had cause to look worried while facing his future, it was this one, for his life had already been complicated by a bloody war and the economic disasters of Reconstruction, and he was now facing the task of building a future and supporting a family with no skill except farming, a precarious business to be getting on with in 1869. *Goodspeed* delicately refers to his education: "[H]is early advantages were limited, owing to the newness of the country at that time,"[1] which undoubtedly means that all the education he got was obtained in a one-room school or, more likely, at his mother's knee. But he wrote a beautiful hand and was an avid reader who added to the library that I have already characterized as the salvation of a bored household until 1942 when my mother gave it to the school.

Joseph H. Jones family, circa 1892. Front row: Mary Margaret, Maggie, Boss, Joseph, Ruth Stroud, and Alfred Stroud. Back row: Sallie, Gordon, Luther, and Irene. *Author's collection.*

The matching picture of his bride Mary Margaret Brown is equally poignant. There is a look of profound sadness in her eyes, as if she had enjoyed little happiness in the past and entertained slight hope for much in the future. And, indeed, their wedding, on October 7, 1869, in Maury County, Tennessee, as we will see later, followed a decade of devastating emotional and financial blows to her family and preceded a life of hard work, poverty, and emotional blows to her and Joseph. The world they faced was not the world they had been brought up to hope for.

Joseph Hubbard Jones was born February 27, 1837, in Nashville, Tennessee, and as I have already mentioned, was moved to Arkansas in early childhood. According to *Goodspeed,* he began farming for himself at the age of eighteen. It is impossible to know exactly what land he was "planting" in 1860 when he is first styled "Planter" in the census, whether he was simply in business with his father or also rented land from someone else, or whether he was, perhaps, tending land for absentee owners, as Uriah had and as he himself did after the Civil War for the rest of his life. Whatever arrangements he had were interrupted by four years of service in the Confederate Army.

Joseph's memoir of his experiences as an infantryman, "Sketch of My Army Life from 1861 to 1865," is an outline of the history of his regiment, First Arkansas Volunteers, which fought, among other battles, Shiloh, Murfreesboro, Farmington, Chattanooga, Chickamauga, Perryville, Lookout Mountain, Missionary Ridge, Resaca, Peach Tree Creek, and Jonesborough. He was in North Carolina with Joseph E. Johnston on May 26, 1865, at the surrender of the Army of Tennessee and made his way home, mostly on foot, arriving by August, when he signed the oath of loyalty to the United States of America to regain his citizenship. Although his style was as terse as he could make it, Joseph was still able to convey some of the misery he had been through as well as some of the wonder, "We went into service right away, principally guarding the Potomac River and building forts. On the 21st day (after enlistment) we were put on a forced march for Bull Run. When we reached the battle field we were held in reserve and were run from hill to hill. We watched the fight nearly all day, but failed to get into the fight at all. It was there we witnessed the first and grandest cavalry charge we ever witnessed." He ends this way, "For four long years I stood the storm of shot and shell; was wounded twice; and was engaged in sixty-four hand fought battles."[2]

The family story is that the war made a man of him; he had matured so much they did not recognize him when he reappeared at the yard gate on his return after four years away. He was of slender build and walked with a cane, perhaps because of his war wounds. The amnesty oath, which he signed with his father, describes him as "6 feet 1 inch tall, light hair and blue eyes, a farmer."[3]

Joseph shows up in public records in February 1868 when his father deeded him the 280 acres mentioned above and again on June 23, 1868, when he borrowed money with a lien on a crop he was taking over from Ira E. Brown and James M. Frierson, on their plantation at Red Fork, which came to be known as the Belco Place.[4] And this is the public record most significant for Joseph's private life because Ira E. Brown was the father of his future wife, Mary Margaret Brown, and James M. Frierson was Mrs. Ira E. Brown's cousin. So Mary Margaret's family and fortunes come into the Jones family story at this point, and they are important for a number of reasons, not the least of which is that ties maintained with Tennessee relatives allowed Mary Margaret and Joseph to send their older children back there for a better education than was available in rural Desha County. It is an interesting fact of the westward migration to Arkansas that the mid-point in the journey, in this case Maury County, Tennessee, became "the old country." Although the first residence in America for this branch of the Frierson family had been in South Carolina from 1730 until 1810, South Carolina seems to have been forgotten by the time they left Tennessee for Arkansas in 1860. There were no tales about South Carolina in our household as I was growing up, although there were many about Tennessee, which was considered "the land of milk and honey." My father remembered with pleasure the time he had been taken there as a small child. The most impressive thing about it was an ancient blind woman who sat all day hunched before the kitchen fire, smoking a pipe. A small black boy was supposed to keep her pipe lit, and to amuse himself and tease her, he would light a stick in the fire and hold it a foot from her face and say, "Puff, Granny. Puff." My father had no idea who the old woman was. (That house, at Ashwood, near Columbia, Tennessee, is still standing.)

On November 15, 1860, Ira E. Brown and James M. Frierson who lived at Ashwood, just south of Columbia in Maury County, Tennessee, bought a thriving plantation in Red Fork Township, including "equipment and 'people,'" from a man named J. W. S. Ridley, also a resident of Maury County, for $132,200. Ridley retained a lien on the property as collateral for the loan of the purchase money.[5] Ridley had bought the property, comprising 825 acres, slaves, and equipment, two years before on December 1, 1858, from Napoleon B. Burrow and his wife Francis for $45,150.[6] The plantation, which stretched from the eastern edge of Belco Lake to the town of Red Fork, is still held as a continuous property, although Red Fork has disappeared without trace. (This place is about three miles from the Jones family farm, as the crow flies.)

Since there is only one piece of property under Ridley's name in Red Fork Township in the 1860 census, it may be assumed that this one, listed in the agriculture schedule under the name Ridley and Long, is the farm that became the Brown-Frierson place on November 15, 1860. There were 600 acres cleared and 260 unimproved, with a value of $50,000. They had $1,500 worth of implements, 2 horses, 29 mules, 6 milch cows, 2 working oxen, 30 other cattle, and 40 swine, with a total value of $4,600. They produced 5,000 bushels of Indian corn, three hundred 400-pound bales of cotton, 30 bushels of Irish potatoes, 300 pounds of butter, and slaughtered animals worth $283. (These figures refer, of course, to the 1859 crop.)

According to the slave schedule, Ridley and Long owned 70 slaves, which goes a long way toward explaining why Brown and Frierson paid as much as they did for the property, if all the slaves were included in the sale. To comprehend this, it is helpful to look at an appraisal made in Chicot County, the county adjacent to Desha on the south, of the 211 slaves on the Bellevue and Yellow Bayou plantations belonging to Junius W. Craig. On July 14, 1860, a court-ordered appraisal was made by three disinterested men for a court suit. The slaves, ranging in age from six weeks to sixty-one years, were divided fairly evenly between males and females. Their average value was determined to be $881, which means that the individual values ranged from $2,800 for a blacksmith to $100 for the youngest child.[7]

Taken on the average, then, of $881 each, the group of seventy slaves would have cost Brown and Frierson $61,670, nearly half their purchase price, which they borrowed almost entirely from the seller. Even if they had bought only twenty slaves with the property (perhaps the minimum number necessary to staff an operation of this size), the price for them could have been as high as $40,000, a considerable investment to be lost in the next few years.

The property, on the south bank of the Arkansas River, was wide open to the depredations of both Federal and Confederate troops. My father remembered the tales told by black people who lived on it during the war of gunboats sailing up and down the river shooting at random out across the fields. According to family legend,

Yankee soldiers burned five hundred bales of Brown and Frierson cotton on the dock at Red Fork, for which my father tried to get compensation in the 1920s, but he could find no witnesses. (It is likely that it was burned by Confederates to harass the Federals with a scorched earth, for not only did the Union need cotton and so would have wanted to take it undamaged but also if the officers in charge of the Federal detachment that chanced upon it happened to be dishonest, a flourishing black market in cotton beckoned.)

Brown and Frierson show up next in the public records on August 11, 1866, giving Thomas Jones, their cotton factor in Memphis to whom they already owed $8,283, a mortgage for money to finish their present and future crops. Times being what they were, it was a desperate measure. The document is worth reading in full because it gives a picture of the operation they had salvaged after the losses brought on by the war. Somehow or other, they had managed to get 530 acres tilled and planted, and there was enough hope left in their world for a cotton factor to give them a credit line of $50,000 against their expectations and everything they owned. Obviously nobody could imagine how much worse things were going to get. To alter slightly Alexander Pope's famous statement on optimism, "Hope springs eternal in the farmer's breast." Here is the document:

> We hereby convey to Thomas Jones his heirs and assigns for the consideration of one dollar to us in hand paid and the other consideration hereinafter named our growing crops of cotton in the State of Arkansas & County of Desha the same being about 450 acres and our corn crop now growing the same being about 80 acres all on our farm & which we are cultivating in said county & state. Also our horses and mules being 23 head our cattle 50 head our stock of hogs being about 150 head. But this conveyance is made for the following uses and trusts and for none other. That is to say we are indebted to Jones Brothers Commission Merchants in the city of Memphis in the sum of seven thousand dollars. And to said Thomas Jones in the sum of one thousand & eighty-three dollars for monies advanced us & for supplies to carry on our farming operations and have the obligations of Jones Brothers to advance us such further sums as may be necessary to mature & get our crop into market and

convert the same into money the whole supplies to be shipped and managed & sold by said Jones Brothers. And whereas said Jones Brothers in order to enable us to complete successfully our farming operations not only this year but for the next years also have agreed to accommodate us with advances to any amounts required by us not to exceed fifty-thousand dollars upon the conditions that we will pledge to convey not only the present crop but the crops of the ensuing years to indemnify them for such advances and convey also our said batch of land for the same purpose and give them the handling & selling of our said crops with the usual rate of commission for so doing & the usual commission & advances ... [we also pledge] all of our said crops our stock & farming tools and our land containing about 700 acres and the same bought by us from J. W. S. Ridley and for full and particular description of which we refer to our bond for title from said Ridley for said land ...[8]

So, it was into this web of tangled affairs that young Joseph H. Jones stepped on June 8, 1868, when he took over Ira E. Brown's crop and mortgaged it to Thos. H. Allen Co., his own cotton factor in Memphis, for $200, money to be used to complete making and gathering the crop. If the loan were paid in full by December 1, 1868, the mortgage would be null and void, which is apparently what happened, because Joseph is not mentioned in the suit filed against Ira E. Brown's estate by James W. S. Ridley and the estate of Thomas S. Jones in October 1869. For Ira E. Brown was dead by that time and so was Thomas Jones, the cotton factor in Memphis who had been so generous with him in the matter of credit in 1866. When the suit was settled in the October 1870 chancery court term, it was revealed that Brown and Frierson still owed Thos. Jones & Co. $8,083 on their line of credit, but far worse than that, they still owed Ridley $131,763 on the original mortgage he had given them for $132,200 when they bought the land, slaves, and equipment in 1860. To complicate matters further, a man named B. F. Grace now claimed title to part of the land because he had bought it at sheriff's sale in May 1868, in a levy against James M. Frierson. The court found that J. W. S. Ridley's lien was "superior to the rights of complainants and defendants" and that he could recover of defendants the sum due, and a special commissioner was appointed to sell the land if the money had not been paid by December 1, 1870. In the April term of chancery court, 1871, it was reported that the lands had been sold back to James W. S. Ridley for $20,000.[9]

Ira Brown may have turned his crop over to Joseph Jones in June 1868 because he was already ill, for, according to the Jones family Bible record of births, deaths, and marriages, he died on November 5, 1868, "aged 49 years 10 months & 28 days." His widow Sarah Elizabeth Frierson Brown took the remnants of her family back to Maury County, Tennessee, whence they had come on this ill-fated move west. In addition to her husband, in the eight years the family had been in the Delta, Sarah Elizabeth had lost four children: her son Gordon Brown, age 16 years, 2 months, and 15 days on September 3, 1861 and her three daughters Amelia Frierson Brown, age 1 year, 9 months, and 9 days on March 4, 1863; Adaliza Brown, age 10 years, 8 months, and 3 days on November 18, 1866; and Martha Armstrong Brown, age 8 years, 9 months, and 20 days on October 4, 1867. The custom of enumerating the days and months as well as the years in the ages of the deceased in these old family records is a poignant reminder of how short lives frequently were and that the records were kept by people mourning their loss.

There is a long list of likely possibilities for what the five members of this family could have died of that includes malaria, typhoid fever, yellow fever, cholera, dysentery, pneumonia, and snakebite, all of which went with the Delta territory. There was no effective control over mosquitoes until 1946 when the United States government instituted a massive spraying program with DDT that virtually eliminated malaria, and water supplies were tainted until 1928 by frequent flooding and human waste, especially since the water table in this area is high enough to provide water in shallow wells routinely used for drinking and washing.[10] The Desha County venture had taken a terrible toll on this family, both emotional and financial. However, two children were born to them while they lived in Arkansas: Amelia Frierson Brown on May 23, 1861, who died before the age of two, and Ira E. Brown Jr. on December 15, 1866, who lived until 1947. When Sarah Elizabeth returned to Tennessee, she took with her the remaining four children: Mary Margaret, age 22; Ella Walton, age 8; Sara Jane, age 16; and Ira E. Jr., age 3.

Joseph Jones was in Maury County, Tennessee, by October 7, 1869, for his wedding to Mary Margaret and was probably still there on June 15, 1870, or thereabouts, when the census taker came to the farm on Pea Ridge, most of which now belonged to him. This would explain his absence from the census rolls. The first page of the pocket book he was carrying at the time lists two addresses: "Jos. H. Jones, Red Fork, Ark., and Jos. H. Jones, Ashwood, Tennessee." It also enumerates his expenses from January until October 1, 1870, including expenses of the trip to Tennessee as $514.75, which, judging from other notes, he seems to have borrowed. Their first child, Irene, was born in Tennessee on November 14, 1870. And Joseph was still in Maury County on January 19, 1871, when he signed a note promising to pay Thomas Jones "two hundred and forty dollars for two horse mules one a black the other a yellow mouse three years old next spring." [11]

When he did get home, perhaps not until after his father died on June 17, 1872, Joseph had staggering problems to face concerning his land. There is no record of Uriah's leaving a will, but presumably Joseph inherited the 160 acres that his father had retained as a homestead when he gave (or sold) Joseph the bulk of his land in 1868. So he already had the 280 acres he had bought from his father in 1868 and since he owned the land outright, his main problem then and for the rest of his life was finding the money to pay the taxes on it.

For most of the years between 1872 and 1906, while he was in charge of the farm, Joseph was able to pay the real estate and levee assessments but sometimes was not, and the threat of losing his land must have been a monster ready to jump out of the shadows of his mind and swallow him before he fell asleep every night of his life. And for good reason. When he inherited from Uriah in 1872, eighty acres were already forfeit from his father's failure to pay the 1871 taxes. In fact, in the thirty-six years of Joseph's management, some or all of the property was forfeited seven times: in 1873, 1877, 1880, 1882, 1883, 1893, and 1905.

And some of the land was lost along the way, but the Jones family never moved. Joseph was usually able to find money to pay the taxes and redeem his land during the two years of grace following forfeiture, and at least twice the farm was saved by the wretched economic conditions that caused him to lose it in the first place. The men who bought it at the courthouse door were unable to pay the taxes either, so it reverted to the state, and Joseph applied for, and received, first on June 28, 1876, and again on April 12, 1883, donation deeds provided by forgiving laws passed by the legislature in the matter of forfeited lands. But the relief brought by the donation certificate on April 12, 1883, for the unpaid taxes of 1873 and 1879 was short lived. On September 19, 1883, he received notice that if he did not pay taxes of $15.62 plus penalties within twenty days, the land would be sold at the courthouse door in Watson on December 20, 1883.

And it was. John N. Moore, John D. Adams, G. W. Sappington, W. I. Turner, and James Murphy bought it together for $41.99, and then John Adams immediately sold half his interest to Wm. E. Stowe for $340. But on December 20, 1885, Joseph paid G. W. Sappington as trustee $53.87 for the taxes, penalty, and accrued interest and got his land back.

There was tax trouble again in 1891. The friendly atmosphere in which these matters were handled is illustrated by the following letter from W. T. Watkins, deputy clerk for the Arkansas City District of Desha County.

> June 9th 1893
> J. H. Jones, Esq.
> Medford, Ar
>
> Dear Sir & Friend
> In reply to yours of June 2nd, 1893. Your lands were sold June 15th 1892 to the Levee Tax of 1891. It will cost you $43.95 to redeem your land that includes the taxes for 1892 and out of this amount you can pay $9.00 in scrip which you can get at 50c there fore it will only cost you $39.45 to redeem the whole of your land. But you will have one year yet to redeem in and you need not be in a hurry. When you get ready you can send me the amount and I will redeem it for you, or you

can come down yourself. It will cost Mrs. Dickinson $20.40 but she can pay $3.20 of this amount in scrip which will make the amount in currency $18.45 for the whole of her land on Pea Ridge adjoining yours, and she also has a year more to redeem in, but I will pay this amount for her and send her the redemption certificate. I would redeem it right now and send certificate but have not got the money now, but will do so soon. I will see that she will not loose [*sic*] her land. I am glad the water did not damage your crop much. I hope you will have luck with your crop this year and make plenty of corn and not loose any of your Hogs. You are pursuing the right course and I hope you will succeed. If only the balance of the people of Desha County would raise their own meat and corn I think they would [be] a great deal better off. We have had a big water here this year, it liked 11 inches of being as high as it was last year, it has commenced to fall here now and has fallen 3 ? inches altogether. My family are all well now and send regards to you and yours. I will be out to see as soon as I get a chance. Give my regards to all your family and also to Mr. and Mrs Stroud. Let me hear from you once and a while.

Your Friend,
Will T. Watkins[12]

Joseph redeemed the land this time on April 26, 1894, with a payment of $61.33 for his 1891 delinquent taxes and penalty as well as his taxes for the years 1892 and 1893. The breakdown of the individual taxes on his redemption certificate from Aunt Sallie's trunk goes this way:

State General	3.10
State School	2.86
Sinking Fund	.72
Pension	.35
County General	7.15
District School, No. 6	7.15
Red Fork Levee	33.30
Costs and Penalty	5.95
Clerk's Fees for 3 Certificates	.75
Total	71.33

The mistake in addition of ten dollars in the state's favor is corrected in another place on the certificate. It would undoubtedly have been noticed by Joseph.

By 1896, Joseph's daughter Sallie was teaching in the Pea Ridge school, and her salary was used to help pay the taxes, without her ever seeing any money. On April 12, 1896, Joseph received the first typewritten communication in the family papers from John Kitely, county clerk:

> Inclosed [*sic*] find tax receipt, I will put in all or what part I can of Miss Sallies warrant, on the final settlement and may be able to get its face value, if so she shall have the full benefit it will be some days before the books are balanced up so I can tell exactly how much can be used."[13]

A "warrant" was a certificate for a teacher's salary. When the county lacked the money to redeem warrants, they were traded at a discount to whoever would take them in lieu of cash.

Joseph routinely mortgaged the farm every spring to get "furnish" money to make a crop, and on April 4, 1905, he mortgaged it to W. D. Preston, sheriff of the county, for five hundred dollars, in a move that was ultimately the family's salvation, as will be seen in the tenure of the next generation.

Putting aside the tax problems during Joseph's tenure, we can look now at the use he made of the land and the kind of living the family got from it. The 1880 population census lists the Jones dwelling house #399 containing Joseph, 44, occupation farming; Maggie, 32, occupation wife and housekeeping; Irene, 9; Sallie V., 7; Gordon H., 4; Luther T., 2; and Chat Fisher, 17, a black farm laborer. All the children except Irene were born in Arkansas.[14]

The 1880 agriculture census for Red Fork Township lists "#5, Jos. H. Jones" with 60 acres tilled and 180 acres woodland; value of farm and buildings, $1,000; value of implements, $25; value of livestock, $325; and cost of building and repairing (in 1879), $30. Amount paid for wages in 1879, $75: laborers white, 6 weeks and laborers black, 8 weeks, exclusive of house work. Livestock: 1 horse, 4 milch cows, 12 other cows, 3 calves dropped, 1 cow purchased, 1 cow slaughtered, and 1 cow died. Eighty-four pounds butter were produced in 1880. On hand for June 1, 1880 were 30 swine, 38 barnyard poultry, and 90 "other" poultry. In 1879 there were 266 eggs produced as well as Indian corn, 8 acres made 80 bushels; cotton, 12 acres made 7 bales; 20 bushels Irish potatoes; 40 bushels sweet potatoes; 40 pounds honey; and 10 pounds wax. Estimated value of all farm production in 1879, $640.[15]

With this rate of production it is easy to see why meeting a tax bill of even a few dollars posed a problem. The farm did not produce much in the way of cash crops, and it is notable that no land was cleared between 1870 and 1880, although Joseph had acquired 80 more acres of woodland. But at his father's death in 1872, Joseph owned 440 acres of land, so he lost 200 acres between 1872 and 1880.

According to steamboat freight receipts in the family papers, cotton and beeswax were shipped to Memphis for sale as well as wool, although no sheep are listed among the farm animals. In considering the matter of cash and the lack of it, it should be remembered that the cows and hogs probably ran in the woods for forage at no cost year round, and according to family legend, all the hay anybody wanted could be cut free on the prairie across the Arkansas River in Arkansas County. It is puzzling that no mules are listed among the farm animals, but it is likely that some of the "other" cows listed were working oxen. My father, born in 1886, remembered that oxen had been used for field work in his childhood.

Since his skills were so limited, there was little aside from farming that Joseph could do to earn money to sustain his growing family, but there were a few activities that may have helped ease his financial strain a little. For one thing, he took care of farming matters for absentee landowners, for an undetermined amount of compensation. One such arrangement was with the William McDowell family in Memphis. The tone of the correspondence is that of a long, friendly relationship that passed down to William's son Wallace, after William died. Money is never mentioned, but a considerable amount of time was required for the things Joseph was asked to do by the McDowells. My father was still in touch with them in the 1930s, although they no longer owned the land adjacent to ours.

Joseph was licensed to teach for six months in 1880, undoubtedly a desperate interim measure on the part of the county school board to find a teacher for the Pea Ridge school, and the appointment could not have paid more than a pittance.[16] From time to time he was asked to collect local bad debts for cotton factors in Memphis, for which he was paid. He occasionally sold a cow. A note from Dr. Louis P. Furbish in Red Fork is interesting for its graceful style and the insight it gives into what could not be bought:

> 3/29/04. Mr. Jones: Please send me a milch cow by hour if possible. It is impossible to buy milk or butter in the neighborhood and very disagreeable to live without them. Very truly yours, L. C Furbish. [17]

He also kept a commissary for the people who worked for him as well as a few neighbors and undoubtedly made a little at that and, in addition, was able to buy necessities for the family at wholesale prices. His supplier was a firm in Memphis, "Toof, McGowan & Co., Grocers, Cotton Factors and Dealers in Levee and Railroad Contractors' Supplies." The prices on their invoices explain a great deal about how the Jones family managed as well as it did with little money:

May 8, 1888.

2 Bbl. Meal		6.00
2 Bbl. Flour		10.50
20 lbs. Soda		1.30
? Box Lakeside Soap		1.75
30 yds. Cotton Plaids		2.40
10 yds. Cottonade		3.75
3 pc. Mosquito Bar (39 yds ea.)		14.04
1 pc. Print (cotton material)		3.60
1 Pc. 4/4 Brown Domestic (40 yds)		3.49
4 Overshirts		2.40
3 Pr. Jeans Pants	(33/33)	4.50
2 Pr. Plow Shoes	(1/8, 1/11)	3.00
2 Pr. Men's Calf Shoes	(1/8, 1/6)	5.50
2 Muslin Undershirts		1.00
1 Brinley Plow		8.00

| 2 Handled hoes | 1.00 |
| Pkg., Dray & Insurance | 2.00 |

On October 26, 1889, Toof, McGowan & Co. wrote Joseph the following note on an invoice for an overcoat costing $7: "This is not as good a coat as you order but it is the best thing we could get of that size in a long coat. The styles are short this year and cost from $15 to $35."

An interesting advertisement sent to Joseph in May 1904 by the wholesale liquor firm of Sandefur-Julian Co. of Little Rock offers seven-year-old " Rosemont" rye whiskey at $3.15 a gallon or "Sunshine Whiskey" at two gallons for $5.00 ("This whiskey is known all the world over for its fine quality, and is well worth double the price we ask.") or, even cheaper, "Three Friends Whiskey" at three gallons for $6.00, "express paid and shipped in plain sealed cases bearing no marks to indicate contents." The prices of this whiskey, so modest by present standards, hint that pleasures were cheap until you look at the list above and realize that for the three dollars that a gallon of good rye would cost a man, he could get two pairs of jeans or a barrel of corn meal.

Although it took little cash to live if you owned your land, the Jones family was poor but so was almost everyone they knew, and many were much worse off than they. It may have been by the skin of Joseph's teeth that they managed to hold on to some of the land and make a life that gave them a respectable position in the community with pleasures and satisfactions as well as hardships, but they did it. And it is doubtful that they spent much time whining about their lot. Hope is the farmer's motivation: "Next year, the weather will be fine, the army worms won't hatch and there'll be such a good crop we can pay our debts and come out ahead." Since this was the outlook in our household in 1936, the nadir of the Great Depression, it is reasonable to believe it was always so.

When we left the personal narrative, Irene, the first born to Joseph and Mary Margaret, had just arrived in Maury County, Tennessee, on November 14, 1870. They had six more children, all born in Arkansas: Sarah Virginia (Sallie), July 5, 1873; Gordon Hubbard, April 17, 1876; Luther Turner, December 31, 1878; Margaret Amanda (Maggie),

November 8, 1882; Ella Elizabeth, April 11, 1885 (died November 9, 1885); and Grover Cleveland (Boss), October 16, 1886 (my father).

The house Joseph built for his family sometime between 1869 and 1872 is the house both my father's generation and my own were born in. In the beginning, it had two large, high-ceilinged rooms on each side of an open, wide dogtrot. At some point this passage was enclosed at each end to make a more useful hall that, along with the porches on front and back, helped keep the house cooler in summer and warmer in winter. One of the two rooms on each side of the hall had a fireplace with a "stick and mud" chimney, made of clay and wood, the cheapest and only locally available materials, there being no stones in the ground. The kitchen was in a separate building off the back porch, attached to the house by a covered walkway, a common arrangement in Southern houses not only to minimize the danger of the perpetual kitchen fire destroying everything in an accident but also to keep the cooking fires from heating up the rest of the house in summer. I do not remember this house, but my brother Jodie, born in 1921, recalls that the back and sides were rough lumber and that the front had been dressed with smooth siding. The roof, of course, was made of hand-hewed cypress shingles, made on the place with a froe. The stick chimneys were in use well into the twentieth century as my brother Grover, who was born in 1912, remembered them. One of them is discernible on the picture of the 1870s house included in this book.

In the beginning, the cooking was undoubtedly done in a fireplace, but by the turn of the twentieth century there was a big wood-burning cookstove. For this house, the kitchen also served as the dining room. Until well into the twentieth century there was also a cook who had come from Tennessee as a slave with the Brown family. Again, one cannot help wondering whether this cook was the woman, Caroline, bequeathed to the adolescent Mary Margaret Brown by her grandmother Margaret Amelia Frierson on September 9, 1859.[18]

The steamboat freight bills for supplies ordered from Memphis had few groceries on them except flour, meal, coffee, and sugar, and the closest store was at Medford, the nearest boat landing a couple of miles away—over a road so muddy as to be frequently impassable to anything but horses, so it is certain that most of the food they ate was raised on the farm. And they were helped by nature in this, as the mild climate and incredibly rich, rock-less soil are the stuff a gardener's dreams are made on. There were Irish and sweet potatoes, collards, turnips and their greens, mustard greens, English peas, several varieties of black-eyed peas (including whippoorwill, crowder, and lady peas), green beans, corn, okra, onions, lettuce, cabbage, cucumbers, watermelons, and cantaloupes. There were tomatoes, also, once it became acceptable to eat them; my mother said that in her childhood they were looked on with suspicion and called "love apples." (Whether they were considered an aphrodisiac she never specified, but the terminology suggests it—and that would certainly have cast suspicion on them as food for respectable folks.)

There were also apples, pears, peaches, cherries, and figs from the orchard as well as wild dewberries, blackberries, elderberries, muscadines, persimmons, black walnuts, hickory nuts, and pecans in season. In the 1930s, during my childhood, there were a few old apple trees and a pear tree left from my grandfather's time, and as I write in 2006, the only one left is the pear tree, now well over a hundred years old, still bearing a few delicious pears every year.

For meat they had chickens, ducks, turkeys, and geese from the yard, pork from their own hogs, occasional beef from a slaughtered cow, fish when someone had time to catch them, and game when anyone had leisure to shoot it. There were abundant wild geese, ducks, turkeys, quail, squirrels, and deer, ranging right up to the yard fence down into my father's generation. All of the men were avid hunters. In spring, summer, and fall—the times of year when hens lay best—they had eggs, and of course there were cows for milk, cream, and butter and honey from wild bees. As a small boy my father had the job of churning, and he recalled thinking at the time that they milked twelve cows just to have something for him to do. He jokingly said he thought all that churning as a child had stunted his growth.

Food was one of their pleasures, and the way things were cooked a matter of pride. So when these products of the garden, orchard, poultry yard, and forest got to the table, they were cooked as close to perfection as possible in the particular style of American cuisine that is an earmark of the South. A Southern cook with a heavy hand is dangerous because, at its worst, this food lies like lead in the stomach. In that house a light touch was prized.

The ingredients, except for pork, had to be eaten fresh because there was no refrigeration before about 1930 when the road was graveled and an ice truck could come out from Dumas once or twice a week, and until well into my father's generation food was not canned. Some things like black-eyed peas, apples, and peaches could be sun-dried and cucumbers were pickled, but for the most part, vegetables and fruits were eaten fresh, when in season. The growing season is mercifully long. Pork could be kept year round because it was salted and smoked and left cured at the end of the process. When hogs were killed in the fall at the first cold snap, there was fresh pork for a few days including sausage, souse, brains, and cracklings made when the fat was rendered for lard. Pigs feet were pickled in brine. Beef was an occasional treat because it could not be kept fresh for long and was not salted or smoked. For this reason, pork formed the center of the cooks' imagination. Everything revolved around it, and a house without a smoked ham in reserve was a poor house indeed. When I say that pork was the center of the cooks' imagination, I mean that it was not only the main dish at most meals but was also used for seasoning vegetables such as peas, beans, and greens, which were traditionally simmered several hours with a piece of pork.

At every meal there would have been fresh bread, either corn bread, biscuits, or both. On special occasions there would have been yeast-rising rolls and "light" bread in loaves eight inches tall. The cookstove had to be kept going almost all day and since it was made of cast iron and not insulated, generated a tremendous amount of heat. Since I have written about Southern food in other places, I will try not to be repetitive here, but the skill it took to make angel food cakes, fluffy biscuits, light rolls, and loaves in the oven of a wood-burning stove bears mention any time this cuisine is discussed.[19]

The 1927 Flood went through that house at a depth of about six feet and washed away the furniture not held together with pegs or bolts and most everything else. I remember the remains of pieces of furniture as well as old clocks and a candle mold lying around the yard in the 1930s. Uriah and Joseph's generations apparently ate off ironstone china because there are still several reverently treated unbroken pieces of it left.

Mary Margaret loved flowers, and a rose bush that came with her from Tennessee threatened to take over the yard for some eighty years. Her daughter Irene is picking a rose from it in a picture from about 1898. This rose bush was large enough in my childhood for the children to make tunnels they could crawl around in, and my brothers and I have cuttings from it in our own yards. It is apparently indestructible and the first rose to bloom every spring. For women like my grandmother, my aunts, and my mother, gardening probably represented more than it does to us, for whom it is a pleasant enough pastime equaled by other pleasures. But in their heavily patriarchal society, this was their space, their portion of the world. From the beginning, the house with its yard was the women's domain, and they took great pride in it. The men were in charge of fields and crops and the decisions they entailed, but the house and gardens belonged to the women—and in this sphere their word was law. Every visit by guests ended with a tour of the flower beds, when cuttings and bulbs were given to anyone who admired them. This was a custom passed from my grandmother's generation down to Aunt Sallie and my mother, who spent every spare hour they had working in the flowers.

Another pleasure the women enjoyed was fine needlework. They made quilts, taking pride in the number of stitches that could be gotten into an inch of "piecing" in the top, and they made their own clothes, paying careful attention to the latest fashions they could keep up with in magazines and pattern catalogs. But they enjoyed and treasured "fancy work" most of all. This was embroidery or "drawn work," as they called the making of lace, and a woman of a certain class was expected to excel at it. "Common" women might know how to make clothes and quilts, but they did not know how to do "drawn work," a skill handed down from one generation to the next and taught, as well, in colleges and "ladies seminaries." The women in this family would make lace on a scrap of flour sack if no other material was available, and they routinely worked the edges of sheets and pillow cases as well as the hems of petticoats and camisoles. There were lace doilies and longer pieces on every surface and antimacassars on the chairs. My mother found "fancy work" restful and could see to do it without glasses until her death. It was frequently a communal activity, as the following letter to Aunt Sallie from her friend Fannie Owen Shaifer indicates:

Hitchcock, Texas
Oct. 31, 1901

My dear girl,

... I am trying to do a little fancy work these days but I progress very slowly ... I want a table cover and I thought of getting a pattern with a linen center and the lace work all around. Wouldn't it be pretty? ... I want to try to make a small cover of drawn linen for a small table I have. ... I do wish you could spend this whole winter with me.

Couldn't you? We could have a pleasant time, and we could do lots of fancy work together.[20]

The men had their pleasures too. During the 1880s, at least, Joseph belonged to a fraternal organization called "Knights of Honor" and was addressed as "Bro." in correspondence from his fellow knights. Along with his friend William McDowell from Memphis, he also belonged to the "Ozark Lake Hunting Club" that owned a hunting preserve on the river. Family legend has it that his love of hunting got in the way of his business and was a reason that the farm did not do better than it did. According to Aunt Mandy, the cook who was still there in 1908 when my mother arrived on the scene, every autumn, when Joseph's friends from Memphis came down to hunt, he would go with them whether his crop was still in the field or not, leaving his wife, Maggie, to worry about it.

Another pleasure the family enjoyed was visiting with a few neighbors with whom they were extremely close. The family's best friends for years were the Coopwoods in Joseph's generation and the Irbys in my father's. These pioneer families settled in the 1840s about three miles east, on the road to Watson. Molly, one of the Coopwood daughters in my grandfather's generation, married Albert Irby, and in my father's generation Benjamin Coopwood's daughter Lulu married Joseph's son Gordon, my father's older brother. Steven Irby, from a different branch of the Irbys, was my father's best friend all his life, and his wife Roberta and their children were our closest friends when I was a child. Benjamin Coopwood was not only Joseph's good friend but also a Confederate veteran who had served in a different unit and with whom Joseph fought over the particulars of certain engagements with the same heat he had fought the Yankees. Although the exact nature of the disagreements has been lost to time, their arguments about the war began immediately after their return, continued until Joseph's death in 1906, and are talked about to this day by descendants on both sides too young to have known either one of them but who have heard about them all their lives. By all accounts, Joseph was one of the mildest, gentlest men alive, but these arguments with Mr. Coopwood are said to have driven him into fits of rage. Both men sported the flowing, fan-like beards considered a badge of honor and identity by Confederate veterans. A Coopwood granddaughter, Hattie Irby Hundley, who was born in 1892, told me in 1980 that when she was a child, the Coopwood and Irby families would pack food and clothes into a wagon and go spend a week at the Jones house. She recalled what good times they all had, singing and dancing late into the night. Music they made themselves was another source of pleasure for these people; most played an instrument of some kind: guitars or fiddles with an occasional bass violin. My father played the violin and thought he would have liked to be a professional musician.

The Cross family lived three or four miles to the west at Pendleton, and although they were not close friends, my father and his brothers and sisters were invited to an annual ball the Cross brothers, Clay and Flournoy, hosted for years. There was a band, champagne was served, and people came from as far away as Tillar, Walnut Lake, and Dumas, a journey of some fifteen miles each way on a dirt road—a long way to go to a dance, but this was a party not to be missed. I think it may have been my father's only experience with champagne. The dancing traditionally went on until dawn when everybody packed up and drove the long miles home.

There were other parties and dances at Red Fork, Arkansas City, and Tillar. The following letter from Aunt Sallie's friend Sallie Owen

Shaifer describes some of the social life and the difficulty of getting
to it over the often flooded and generally impassable roads.

Greenlaws, Tenn
June 8, 1893

My Dear Girl,

    . . . We have been here since Sunday. Sister C's school closed
Wednesday night the 31st when Mr. Shaifer and I went out. We
went from Ark. City for about 2 mi. in a skiff then from there
to 2 mi. beyond Trippe on a hand car, went through water 6 in.
deep just pouring over the track then from there to McGehee
in a wagon and from McGehee to Tillar on the train, didn't we
have a time getting there. I know Mrs. Jones will say I'm a daisy.
Well, we got to Tillar about three o'clock and Sister C and some
of the girls met us at the Depot, we all went to the Church and
stayed until they finished fixing it then we went over to Mrs.
Tillars and at 7:30 all went to the Concert and Sallie it was just
splendid. They had music, dialogues, recitations etc. and the fan
drill. It was about twelve girls, small ones all dressed in red with
red shoes and stockings and fans and they went through all kinds
of motions using the fans and kept perfect time to music. After
the Concert was over we all went up to the hall and danced.
Uncle P Sister C and Mr. S[haifer] and I left at 12. The next day
we all came as far as we could by train then came the rest of the
way 8 mi. in a skiff [back to Arkansas City]. We were real tired
when we got to Sallies about dark. [Sallie is her sister-in-law in
Arkansas City.] Sallie and the children were all so glad to see
Sister C. We had a nice supper and enjoyed it too. You know
Sallie is at the hotel now and the hall upstairs is a splendid place
to dance. Sallie had scoured it out nice, had chairs all sitting
around and about 8 o'clock both Jackson girls Louie Belse
Charlie Lacy and another fellow can't spell his name and Mr. S.
came and we danced until 12:30, had two kinds of cake and ice
lemonade. All enjoyed themselves, and we told them goodbye
for we left the next day. Sister C and I stayed with Sallie and the
next day at noon the boat came. The "Chickasaw" you've seen
her. We went down and got on and left about 2 o'clock that was
Friday and got to Memphis Saturday night but did not get off
until after breakfast Sunday morning. We had a pleasant trip up

and enjoyed ourselves emensely. We went to the Gayoso Hotel the nicest in Memphis went to the Episcopal Church, came back and ate dinner and everything was so good and we ate so much we had to go to our room and loosen up and lay down.... They had buttermilk and I drank a glass of it. You know everything is so fine you hardly know what you are eating and my sis and I are not use to such you know so I thought I'd take a glass of milk because I did know what that was and was somewhat used to such.[21]

Another pioneer family close enough to visit were the Calvin Strouds. Calvin Stroud's son Alfred married Joseph's daughter Irene after the death of his first wife and became an intimate member of the family during my father's youth.

Joseph was in charge of the Pea Ridge school during those years, and here, from his pocket book, is a list of the pupils with their ages for the year 1901.

Bennie Irby	11 years
Hattie Irby	9 "
A. Z. Irby	7 "
Cornelia Coopwood	17 "
Alice Canady	10 "
Hugh Canady	8 years
Stephen Irby	20 "
Grover C. Jones	16 "
Arthur Fillyaw	15 "
Lou Bill Fillyaw	12 "
Ed Pierce	18 "
Ola Stroud	12 "
Ruth Stroud	8 "
Joe C. Stroud	6 "
Mullin A. Watkins	
Bessie Watkins	
Will G. Watkins	

A group of seventeen scholars ranging in age from six to twenty would be a challenge for any teacher, which may be the reason so many were called upon to do it and so few lasted long in the job. The older children in the Jones family were sent to Tennessee to

stay with their Grandmother Brown while getting a bit more education, and at least one, Sallie, attended Henderson-Brown College,
a Methodist institution at Arkadelphia. My father was bitter that he
was the only child not sent off for education. They were so attached
to him—the baby—that they could not bear the thought of part-
ing with him. An indication of this fondness was Sallie's response to
his perceived need of her when he fell down as a child and broke
his leg. Set by a drunken doctor, the limb did not seem to be heal-
ing properly, and the child was in constant pain, so Sallie quit college and came home to nurse him. The story was that the doctor
had wrapped the leg in cotton with the seeds still in it before apply-
ing the cast. On removal of the cast it was found that the seeds had
sprouted and grown, and this was the cause of the incredible pain
to the little boy. Sallie never left home again and continued to take
care of him as best she could, even after his marriage and in the face
of what she considered my mother's interference for the rest of her
life. When my mother married him, he had never washed his own
hair! And of course Aunt Sallie lived with us until she died in 1936.
Since she owned the land and house, it is more accurate to say that
we lived with her. There is some truth in her vision of things: it was
her home, after all, and my mother was simply somebody who had
married into the family. She willed her share of the land to my
father, but that comes into the story of the next generation.

The census records for 1890 have been destroyed, and the census bureau had stopped making individual farm surveys by 1900.
But the population schedule for 1900 shows the following for
Joseph's household, #150: Joseph H. Jones, 63, farmer; Margaret, 53,
housewife; Sallie V., 26; Gordon, 24, farm laborer; Luther, 21, farm
laborer; Maggie A., 17, attending school; and Grover C., 13.[22] So
Joseph and Mary Margaret still had all their children under their
roof except the oldest, Irene, who was married to Alfred Stroud and
lived nearby. And the boys were working the farm.

The much faded family photograph taken about 1892 included
in this book first brought to mind the Thomas Hardy poem that I
chose for the title and epigraph to this narrative. The cherubically
smiling Joseph, with a neatly trimmed beard and the ends of his

moustache curled, sits surrounded by his brood. He is holding his granddaughter Ruth Stroud on his knee; little "Boss," my father, about eight years old, bare-footed, in knee breeches and a ruffled shirt with flowing bow tie, stands between Joseph and Mary Margaret, holding his mother's hand—which, by the way, looks exactly like my hands. Maggie, the youngest daughter, kneels just behind Boss, and the older sons and daughters stand in the back row. On Joseph's left sits his son-in-law Alfred. Even Mary Margaret looks more pensive than sad—unusual for her. It is a picture of contentment. And, indeed, they were enjoying an eighteen-year moratorium on death in the immediate family that lasted from April 1885 when they lost their six-month-old daughter Ella until February 1903 when they lost daughter Irene at thirty-two, a very long stretch in that time and place. But in the three years between Irene's passing and Joseph's own death on March 13, 1906, one blow after another fell on the old man.

When Irene died, her three small children—Ruth, age eleven; Joe, age eight; and Frierson, age two—came to live in the Jones household. It is unclear whether their father Alfred moved or not. His farm was nearby, and it may be that he remained in his own home. There was more illness that year in the Jones family; it may have been the year my father remembered when they all had typhoid fever. Luther was sick enough with something to require a visit by Dr. Robertson from Red Fork every day in August, according to the bill which was still unpaid the following April.[23] Then, one day in October 1903 when Alfred Stroud had not been home for three days, Luther, sent to Red Fork to fetch him, found him drunk in a saloon and with great difficulty persuaded him to return home. As they started to mount their horses, a scuffle ensued in which Alfred stabbed Luther in the back, severing his liver, a wound that killed him on October 30, 1903. Legend has it that Gordon Jones was in the tavern with Alfred, also drunk. They had been arguing, and the knife blow that killed Luther was aimed at Gordon and hit Luther by mistake. At any rate, Luther died. On the advice of the judge, Alfred was sent away to save the family from the disgrace and pain of a trial, and the three Stroud children were left to be raised in the Jones household. (Alfred was back in time for the 1910 census, where he is listed as living in Watson with his son Joe, who was fourteen by then.) Then on March 25, 1905, Mary Margaret died, leaving Joseph with a house full of children and grandchildren, the pet of all being little Frierson Jones Stroud who died of acute indigestion on October 28, 1905, at the age of four!

While the old man was receiving one emotional blow after another, his financial woes were unremitting as well, as the following letter received in February 1904, indicates:

> 2/11/04
> Mr. J. H. Jones
> Medford, Ark.,

Dear Sir:

We thank you for your very prompt answer of the 6th inst. We have just been to the State Land Office and find the tract in question, S.W. 1/4 Sec. 12, Twp. 9 S. R. 3 W. forfeited to the State for the taxes of 1882. The State deeded same to the Red fork Levee Board and on the 31st day of March, 1902, the Red Fork Levee District, by A. Wynn, Pres. Deeded same to Clifford B. Wright, J Gordon R. Wright and Jno. M. Pattison. This deed was recorded on the 2d day of Apr, 1902, at 5 o'clock, P. M. At Dumas, on Record Book volume D, Pages 378–379–380–381–382.

You will see from this that the information given you by Judge Pindall is wrong. We are acting as agents for Wright and Pattison in this matter. Wright and Pattison bought this land from the Red Fork Levee Board and paid for it and, of course expect to get it. You can not blame them for wanting it.

In looking over Mr. Brewer's report we find that he states there is a portion of this in a field and that the land is good and it was from this report that we judged it is a valuable farm. Do not think for an instant that it is our intention to try to hold you up for one cent but kindly look at the matter from Wright and Pattison's stand point.

They bought and paid for it and of course if their title is best will expect to get it and if your title is best we presume you will get it but so far as we, individually, are concerned we had always rather compromise differences than to have law suits. We would advise that you look over this matter carefully and write us what you intend to do, and oblige,

Yours truly,

Yowell & Williams[24]

Apparently this land was truly lost, as it was not listed as collateral for a mortgage by Joseph's son Grover Cleveland (Boss) in 1908 when he listed the other parcels of land in his father's undivided estate. It must have seemed to Joseph that he was losing everything dear to him, both family and property, and he was desperate for money.

So, on April 4, 1905, Joseph, now a widower, mortgaged 160 acres to W. D. Preston for $500 with the understanding that the money could be paid back at any time and the mortgage voided. Joseph was to keep the property up and the taxes paid. Bill Preston was the sheriff and collector of Desha County, a friend of the Jones family and an ardent admirer of "Miss Sallie," Joseph's daughter. His was the hand of fate that saved the farm, as things turned out, but as I have already stated, this is part of the story of the next generation.

Joseph H. Jones died on March 13, 1906, one year and ten days after the death of his beloved Maggie. His estate, the land still mortgaged to Bill Preston, went in five undivided portions to his remaining children, Sallie, Gordon, Maggie, and Boss, and to Irene's children, Ruth and Joe Stroud. He was buried next to Mary Margaret and their children Ella and Luther in the family cemetery, which is a stone's throw from the site of Uriah and Sarah's house.

Goodspeed's description of Joseph in 1890 seems a fitting epitaph:

> He is a man of quiet habits, but of an honest and generous disposition, and is highly esteemed by his many acquaintances and friends. He and wife are members of the Methodist Episcopal Church, South, and take an active part in church work. Mr. Jones is a Democrat, has held the office of Justice of the peace of Red Fork Township for three years, and socially is a member of the Masonic fraternity and K. of H.[25]

CHAPTER 4

The Boss and Sallie Generation

1906–1957

t Joseph's death, the torch passed to his daughter Sallie and to Boss, his youngest son and my father, both single members of Joseph's household at the time of his death. The passage of the land from Joseph to the next generation naturally included the accompanying financial problems, which were complicated by the tangle he left in his last mortgage, made to W. D. Preston on April 4, 1905, for $500. This open-ended mortgage could be paid off at any time with the title reverting to Joseph and his heirs. But Joseph died in 1906, and since the mortgage had not been paid by November 28, 1910, the full 160-acre plot, consisting of the eastern half of the northwest quarter of S13 T9 R3W and the western half of the northwest quarter of S13 T9 R3W, was sold by Preston at the courthouse door to the highest bidder, Henry Saine, husband of Joseph's youngest daughter, Margaret Amanda (Maggie), for the sum of $857.31. On December 9, 1910, Henry Saine sold 80 acres of it back to Preston for $428.65, who promptly, on the very same day, gave it to Aunt Sallie for her natural life with an accompanying mortgage to be held by him until paid, at which time she

Grover
Cleveland
"Boss"
Jones.
Wedding
picture,
1909.
*Author's
collection.*

Zena Cason
Jones.
Wedding
picture,
1909.
*Author's
collection.*

Boss, seated at right, with his one-thousand-pound hammer for building bridges, sometime between 1915 and 1927. *Author's collection.*

would receive title to the eastern half of the northwest quarter of section 13.[1] Boss was left without an acre.

Family legend has it that Preston, who was the sheriff and collector of the county at the time, said that he did it because he could not bear the thought of Miss Sallie Jones being without a home. Another gift from Bill Preston to Aunt Sallie was a beautiful gold pendant watch with her monogram on the fob. Pasted inside the back case there is a printed scrap of paper with the message, "Absence makes the heart grow fonder." My father liked to tell about the time that Bill Preston and some other men were watching a load of fruit from South America being unloaded at Arkansas City, a port town some twenty miles away. One of the men said, "Bill, why don't you send Miss Sallie some fresh fruit?" "Well," he said, "I think I will," and bought an entire bunch of bananas, which was slipped into a burlap bag for the journey in a wagon. He hired a black man to haul the

Farm houses built in 1870 and 1933. *Author's collection.*
  above: a. Sallie taking a bead in front of the 1870 house.
  below: b. The 1933 house.

The family warriors home from World War II, 1946. Ted Willis, Grover Jones, Bob Jones, Jodie Jones, and Bill Lloyd. *Author's collection.*

fruit to our house, who on the way met a friend who was going by there on a mule and decided to save himself the trip. So they loaded the bananas on the back of the mule, behind the saddle. It was a scorching hot day, and Daddy said when the present arrived, it was a tow sack full of mashed bananas! The Jones family thought highly of Bill Preston, even before he saved their land. Neither Sallie nor he ever married; nobody now alive remembers hearing why they never married each another.

The arrangement with the mortgage was all well and good until Preston was killed in a shootout in the line of duty on September 26, 1911, leaving no will but three siblings, Richard A. Preston, Maude Preston Coburn, and Belle Preston Brown, who were not disposed to surrender the title easily, even when the money had been found to pay off the mortgage. The matter was not settled until August 27, 1918, when the Preston heirs gave Sallie V. Jones title in return for her payment to them of $428.65.

Family feeling was undoubtedly complicated by the fact that Richard Preston had married Ruth Stroud, Boss and Sallie's niece, in 1909 and so had a special interest in the matter.[2]

Once her land was securely hers, Sallie made a will appointing her brother, Grover C. Jones, executor and leaving him and his children everything she owned. She never mortgaged the land again, and neither did my father, in his turn. Although in March 1908 he had mortgaged his "undivided ⅙ interest" in his deceased father's estate for $200, presumably to put in a crop—he never did so again.[3] The chattel mortgages in the family papers indicate that they mortgaged everything else for money to make the crops, but both seem to have learned from their grandfather's and father's experience the fate of land that gets mortgaged on the expectation that crop proceeds will pay off the note. Although faced with formidable problems in paying their taxes, which, indeed, fell delinquent in 1926, 1929, and 1932, they were able to pay each time before forfeiture proceedings had to be instituted.[4]

The danger implicit in mortgaging land was a lesson their sister Maggie and her husband Henry Saine had to learn for themselves. After a series of mortgages that they began taking out in 1916 grew progressively larger, they finally lost their eighty acres by foreclosure to the Federal Land Bank in 1929. At that time, Boss bought it back, soon realized he could not pay for it, and returned it. (Without the family's extensive experience in the risks of mortgaging land, Boss and Sallie might have been tempted to mortgage the land they owned to purchase this parcel they so wanted.) Maggie's eighty acres passed through several different hands before my brother Grover eventually bought it back. This land was important to us for several reasons, not the least of which was the presence on it of our family cemetery in which we had continued to bury in spite of its ownership outside the family. Allowing us to bury there and reserve that graveyard for our use alone was a courtesy on the part of its successive owners. Eventually, in 1955, Boss bought the cemetery back from the Lawrence Patton family, who owned the place by then, and in 1976, Grover bought the rest of the land, minus two lots reserved by the Patton families for their homes.

At the time she paid off the note to the Prestons and received title to the land in 1918, Sallie was 45-years old, well-launched into spinsterhood, and a member of her brother Boss's family, in their father's house, where she remained until the day she died, January 21, 1936. In the 1910 census Boss is listed as head of household #262, consisting of G. C. Jones, age 24; Zena, wife, age 21; and Sallie V., sister, age 35.[5] In the 1920 census he is listed as head of household #376, consisting of Grover C., age 33; Zena, age 30; Grover C., age 8; Paul, age 5; Pauline, age 2½; and Sallie, age 44.[6] The family was growing and would continue to do so through May 10, 1931, when I was born.

My father did not particularly like his name, "Grover Cleveland." I think it embarrassed him to have been named for a president, and he always signed it "G. C. Jones." However, he was given the nickname "Boss" while still a baby; legend has it that his father would bounce him on his knee and say, "This is the real boss around here," and the name stuck. Family and friends, including my mother and Aunt Sallie, never called him anything else. People outside the family's circle of friends often assumed he had earned the name by his authority as a stern manager. Not so—he was, rather, a mild-mannered, funny man, a master storyteller who could make a trip to the mailbox interesting. Furthermore, the people who worked for him invariably called him "Mr. Jones." To have called him "Boss" would have assumed a familiarity not held by any employee. He was only about five feet nine inches tall, but he had an air of authority, in spite of his modest stature, that nobody wanted to question. Bob remembers an incident putting up hay one day when two huge field hands, arguing over who was not pulling his weight in stacking bales on a wagon, jumped to the ground ready to kill each other with bale hooks. Boss stepped between them and said they ought to be ashamed of themselves for acting like children. They went back to work without another word. Yet, I do not think I ever heard him raise his voice; he certainly did not in dealing with his family. Like everyone else in the household, he was an avid reader of whatever he could get his hands on. The only thing he did for pleasure that I recall was hunt quail—he was a better shot than either of his two sons who hunted—and this interest meant that there were always handsome bird dogs, usually Llewellyn setters, around the yard. By the time I was old enough to be getting to know my father, the Great Depression and drought were in full swing, and he was immersed in constant, unremitting worry that made him somewhat forbidding to me. Mother constantly cautioned us to be quiet and not disturb him as he sat on the porch in his rocker that had been his father's also, smoking one cigarette after another, as he gazed out over the parching fields.

The nature of the financial arrangement between Boss and Sallie has been lost forever. She owned the land, and he farmed it in the expectation of owning it himself someday, if he outlived her. But how they shared the proceeds is a mystery. The chattel mortgages given for "furnish money" to make the crops were negotiated in his name alone. According to the mortgage he gave D. O. Porter, trustee for the Bank of Dumas on March 26, 1908, in addition to his one-fifth interest in the land he mortgaged the crop expected from 45 acres of cotton and 25 head of cattle, branded with the family brand, "a swallow fork and underbit in right ear and split and underbit in left ear." (Since cattle were allowed free range, they had to be branded.) The papers for the chattel mortgages executed every year for money to put in the crop reveal some details about the farming operation. The chattel and crop mortgage made on March 5, 1925, to the Desha County Bank at Watson reveals that Boss was farming not only Sallie's land but also that belonging to his sister Maggie and her husband Henry Saine—and apparently other acreage as well, for the collateral laid down to obtain a loan of $4,500 included the expected proceeds of 150 acres planted in cotton and 60 acres of corn as well as 8 mules (all he owned), 2 horses, all farming implements (including tools and wagons), and his life insurance worth $2,000.[7]

The income from the forty-five acres of cotton he planted in 1908, about the same cotton acreage his father had usually planted, would have been enough in good years for a meager living for Sallie and Boss and then, after 1909, for them and his wife and growing family. But it was not as good a living as he wanted, and indeed, he said in later years that he had not wanted to be a farmer at all. He did it because somebody had to. So, in addition to farming, he became the bridge builder for Desha County. Nobody recalls how he learned to do this, but from about 1915 until 1927, he was in charge of constructing sturdy timber bridges over the existing bayous and then the canals being dredged for the Cypress Creek Drainage District, formed in 1911 for the system that eventually drained the swamps and made

Desha County prime farming land. He owned his equipment, including a pile driver with a one-thousand-pound trip hammer designed to be hoisted up a scaffold by mules pulling a rope through a pulley and then dropped when a workman sitting on top of the scaffold pulled a trip. All his equipment except the hammer was washed away in the 1927 Flood, and that was stolen before the mud dried and things got back to normal.

Thus ended his bridge-construction career, but during the years he could count on it, this work allowed the family a level of comfort they would not have had otherwise. For example, on July 24, 1918, he bought the family's first automobile, a six-cylinder Oakland, for $1,150 from the McNeely Motor Company in Arkansas City. He paid $750 down and gave McNeely a note for the remaining $400, due December 12, 1918. Then in 1922, he bought a Ford touring car from the same dealer for $557 with half paid down and the rest in 12 equal payments of $23.21.[8] Since farm income is tied to the harvest, or sometimes in the Delta to "Furnish Day," March 1, a man totally dependent on it would have had difficulty meeting monthly payments. The bridge work gave him the means to do it. With the roads in the condition they were in at the time, owning a car must have been a limited pleasure. Few roads in Desha county had been graveled in 1918, and certainly none in Red Fork Township. Furthermore, in wet weather the alluvial soil is bottomless, and some of it called "gumbo" is as sticky as glue when wet and dries on feet and wheels to a cement-like hardness. In dry weather, the dust would have been a foot deep in places. But everyone wanted a car, and I know it gave my father great pleasure to be able to provide one for his family. He talked about that Oakland until the day he died. The road in front of the house, which went from Dumas to McGehee through Watson, was graveled in 1930 and blacktopped in about 1953. Before 1930, according to Grover, it took a half day to get to Watson, six miles away, and a whole day to travel the twelve miles to Dumas!

There were other small additions to income through the years. For example, when the North Memphis, Helena and Louisiana Railroad was being constructed shortly after the turn of the century, Boss had a contract to supply beef to the construction crew.[9] Like most farmers, he was a good carpenter and sometimes turned his hand to building houses for other people. Sallie sometimes worked at the drug store in Watson, and the Jones household, when it was not providing the local schoolteacher, provided the boarding place for the ones who came from elsewhere for the term. In 1908, my mother, Miss Zena Cason, age twenty, came from Fountain Hill in the next county over to teach, first in the Watson school and then at Pea Ridge where she boarded in the Jones household. She and Boss were married on January 4, 1909, in McGehee. (In December 1953, home from Washington University for the Christmas vacation and to get married, I went to Wolchansky's Dry Goods Store in McGehee to buy a wedding suit and was served by the same clerk who recalled with pleasure selling my father *his* wedding suit in 1909!)

Boss and Zena's first child was stillborn, but they had six more who lived to adulthood and, in addition, informally adopted an infant boy, Zena's nephew Ted Willis. The children, in order of appearance, were Grover Cason, January 10, 1912; Paul, August 8, 1914; Pauline, February 23, 1917; Joseph Gallatin, August 14, 1921; Theodore Willis, May 8, 1923; Robert Edward, July 7, 1926; and Mary Margaret, May 10, 1931. Paul died of rheumatic fever on August 14, 1931; the others, except Grover and Ted, are still alive as I write in 2006.

If the Civil War was the major disaster for this farm and its owners in the nineteenth century, an equally threatening incident in the twentieth was the 1927 Flood, followed shortly by the stunning blows of the Great Depression and its accompanying drought. Our farm was about a mile and a half from the Pendleton Break, one of the largest ruptures in the Arkansas River levee and directly in the line of the current. The family was not prepared for it because they did not believe it would reach them. Since the house and farm are situated on an old bluff, in the almost eighty years they had been on Pea Ridge, water from "overflows" had never gotten deep enough to come inside the house, so they expected the threat of this one to pass them by as well. It did not. My brother Jodie remembers it this way:

> The 1927 Flood is still a vivid memory, though I was only
> five years old. . . . It was normal for water to get up high on
> the levee on the river side. Some years it was hard to farm close

to the levee because water would seep under it and come up like springs a half mile or so away. Every tenant house had a hand-operated pump to provide household water. When water was high on the levee some of these pumps would turn into artesian wells with a stream of water squirting out like it was under pressure.

We knew the river was extremely high, but Daddy wasn't too concerned. The river flooded in 1916 and since our house was on the highest point around, water ran through the yard, but of course caused no damage. Late one afternoon an airplane flew low over the house a few times, as if the pilot was trying to tell us something. Airplanes were rarely seen in those days so we were sure he was telling us the levee had broken. I remember the sound the plane made. I don't think I have ever heard the same sound again. Daddy was concerned enough that he dragged a small boat he kept in the lake up to the front yard. Otherwise it was a normal evening. We went to bed as usual and about two o'clock two black men woke Daddy up and asked him if he was going to lie there and drown in his sleep. By this time water was lapping under the house. He had heard it and thought it was raining. . . .

When daylight came, water was as far as you could see. Work immediately started on knocking planks off the barn and building scaffolds to put furniture on and to get us out of the water. We spent the night on the scaffolds and a bootlegger came got us in his motor boat in the morning. Bootleggers were the only owners of motorboats and without their assistance, I don't know what would have happened to us.

The trip to the levee was uneventful. It is hard to imagine the thoughts Mother must have had at this time. The children ranged in age from one to fifteen and we were unloaded on the levee without any food or shelter in sight. The levee was a beehive of black people in the same condition as we were. One sight that struck me was the swiftness of the river as it raced to the break in the levee. . . .

We had been on dry land a short time when Mr. Holcomb came by and took us to his home. His house was one of the old plantation homes that were built before the levees were constructed, and the floor was about six feet above ground level and didn't flood. Mrs. Holcomb and their daughter Bitsy had been moved to higher ground; we spent about three weeks with Mr. Holcomb. [This was J. N. Holcomb, who, at the time, owned the Haywire Farm, the plantation adjoining our farm on the north.] When the water began to recede, Daddy would paddle back to our house to start a cleanup. It was also necessary to cut fences and float the dead animals away. Since our home site was the high spot in the county, livestock naturally found their way there as the water rose. About sixty drowned. I think I can remember seeing cattle bunched up along the fence as we were leaving.[10]

When the water had receded enough, the family returned to the house that was, miraculously, intact and began cleaning up. The water mark on the walls was six feet up, and there was a foot of silt on the floors. After a few weeks, it was decided that Zena and the children should go to Monticello, some forty miles away and in the hills where it had not flooded, to live with her parents and sister Mary Campbell and family for a while and that Boss should go to Arkansas City to work as a carpenter rebuilding flood-damaged houses. They did not return home to Pea Ridge until after Christmas, where there was no school until the next autumn.

So no crop at all was made in 1927, and it is difficult to see how the family managed to hang on and plant the 1928 crop. Again, owning the land they worked was a key factor, for it meant that they could survive as long as money could be found to pay the taxes—already delinquent for 1926, before the levee broke and the flood came in April 1927—and to put in the crop in March 1928. It is ironic that the heaviest tax burden for them was the drainage tax assessed to develop a system of canals that would prevent flooding and make more wetlands arable! Paying those taxes almost broke them, but in our household the system was appreciated. My father would not take part in local efforts to put an end to construction of the canals and the subsequent taxes to pay off the bond issues that were floated to pay for them. Somehow the delinquent taxes were paid in 1928 and in the terrible years following, which of course included the 1929 stock market crash and the subsequent Great Depression as well as the crippling drought in 1930. After the flood, the Red Cross gave Boss a pair of mules to start over with, which he did, dependent by then solely on the farm, as he had lost his bridge-building equipment and business.

As for food, Mother said that the blackberries that grew after the flood were the biggest and juiciest they ever had. I believe it was during those few weeks after the water receded when they stayed home to clean up before going to Monticello that the family ate crawfish for the only time anyone could ever remember doing so.

But there was even hope enough to be mustered by the fall of 1929 for Boss to make a commitment to buy back the 80 acres that his sister Maggie and Henry Saine had lost to the Federal Land Bank in June of that year. The bank foreclosed on June 24, 1929, and the land was immediately purchased by Claude and Gertrude McKennon for $2,625, via a mortgage with the land bank for $2,000.[11] On November 8, 1929, Boss signed an agreement to buy the land for $2,625 from the McKennons to be paid in the following manner: $625 down and a note for $2,000 at 10% per annum to be paid in installments of $200 plus interest every November 1 until the principal should be paid.[12] Today, $32.80 per acre for this prime land looks like a bargain, and indeed it probably was. But Boss farmed it for only one year before realizing he could not make the payments and gave it back. The family story relates that Claude McKennon, a longtime friend of my father, protested that he had never taken a man's land and was not about to begin, but Boss knew it was useless to try to buy it just then and in 1930 insisted on giving it back.

I think it was a concern of Sallie's, as I am certain it was of my parents, that in spite of her will made in 1918, in the event of her death, somehow or other there might be some question about ownership of the land we depended upon. In any case, on July 17, 1933, Sallie gave Grover C. Jones Sr. and his children a warranty deed for an undivided one-half interest in her 80 acres "not to be divided however during the lifetime of grantor S. V. Jones."[13] This land remained in Sallie's name alone on the tax books until her death in 1936. When her will was probated in April 1936, Boss and his children became the owners of the entire 80 acres, the eastern half of the northwest quarter of S13 T9 R3W.

Boss, by this time, was fifty years old, the sole support of a wife and six children, and, without a piece of luck that had come his way just the year before in 1935, would not have been in possession of one foot of land besides the eighty acres left him by his sister. But a bit of good fortune had come his way, and he had taken advantage of it. Like his father and grandfather before him, he also handled business matters for absentee landlords, one of whom was a Memphis lumber man named Richard H. Bodine, who owned a 320-acre farm adjoining ours on the west. Much of this land was in woods, but there were some good fields on it that Bodine rented to various people until 1935. My father kept an eye on this place, sold the cotton, paid the taxes, etc., for Bodine. For this he received a commission of 10 percent of the proceeds of the crops.[14] After a particularly frustrating experience with a tenant who would not keep the fences and houses repaired, Bodine agreed to rent this farm to Boss for five years at the rate of $400 the first year, $500 each for the next two years, and the remaining two years at a sum agreeable to both at the beginning of the fourth year. Boss was to repair the fences, make the houses livable, and clear ten acres of new ground per year.[15]

Renting this additional land raised the family's expectations a notch or two. The cleared portions, weather and insects permitting, could be expected to pay the rent and turn a profit. But this was not all. Bodine also owned 160 acres of timberland bordering a swamp called Round Brake directly south of our farm, not contiguous but close. Though practically inaccessible in bad weather, it had the potential for becoming fine farmland some day. The taxes had not been paid on it since 1927, so it had been forfeited to the state in 1928. Bodine offered it to my father for the payment of the delinquent taxes. Of course he accepted, making the $19.69 payment due for 1927 on October 8, 1935, after which Richard Bodine gave him a quitclaim deed on November 20, 1935. He made the final payment of $98.20 for delinquent drainage taxes on March 23, 1937.[16]

The gift of that 160 acres was more than "a bit of luck," and Bodine's remark in the letter accompanying the quitclaim deed was prophetic, "I hope you make a lot of money out of this property." Over the years the family has indeed made a great deal of money as a consequence of owning that land for a very short time because what Boss did was sell it within three years to F. W. Rana for $1,600, enough money to make a down payment on the 320 acres he was renting from Bodine and clear forty acres of woods on the property to make more arable land. Moreover, Round Brake was covered with old-growth hardwoods, and before selling it Boss and Grover borrowed a sawmill from Stephen Irby, set it up in the woods, and sawed enough lumber to build tenant houses to shelter the labor they needed for their expanded operations. All the boys, as well as Pauline's husband Bill, worked on this lumber project and remembered it the rest of their lives as terrible, surely the hardest physical labor any of them ever did.

On December 7, 1938, Bodine wrote my father to inform him that he would like to sell his 320 acres but that if Boss could not manage to buy it just then, he could continue to rent it at the rate of $650 for 1939 and then $1,000 for 1940, after which it would be put on the open market. He explained that he was raising the rent because my father could now "expect a payment from the government," presumably for *not* raising cotton on some of the acreage. It would clearly be advantageous to own this property, so they reached an agreement whereby Boss, in partnership with Grover, would pay a total of $9,600 for the property with Bodine retaining mineral rights for twenty years in lieu of interest. Following the immediate down payment of $600, there would be twelve payments of $750 each due on November 1 for twelve years. With the proceeds from the sale of the property on Round Brake available for the down payment, the deal was quickly struck.[17]

When they took it on, there was no question that the Bodine Place was fine land and could reasonably be expected to pay for itself, yet the times were so bad that within two years Grover was sure that it would not, that they would never be able to make the payments, and that they should get rid of it. My father, confident that they had done the wise thing, refused to sell, and time proved him right. At what must have been the lowest point in Grover's life, he decided to leave the farm and go off to take a job as carpenter in construction work at Camp Polk, Louisiana, for the then incredible wage of a dollar an hour. The work and living conditions were not to his liking, however, and he was back within a few months to remain until the draft caught him in 1942 and, then after the war, for the rest of his life.

The purchase of the Bodine Place was the beginning of the partnership between Boss and Grover, called "G. C. Jones & Son," that lasted until shortly before Boss's death. Grover was twenty-six years old at the time they formed it, still single and living at home. Thus began the legal aspects of the eventual passing of the farming operation down to the next generation. It was a formality, for there had never been any question that Grover would be the next farmer. And although it would be his tenure that carried the farm into the modern world, steps toward transition had begun by the time he and Boss began their joint venture, for the 1930s fostered the beginning of the mechanical revolution in cotton farming that culminated in the replacement of people with machines and emptied the Delta of thousands of inhabitants.

The beginnings on our farm sound inauspicious: the simple replacement of a plow called a "double shovel" with a one-row cultivator pulled by a pair of mules. But the snowballing consequences were momentous. My brother Jodie's perspective on this time is especially valuable because he not only worked some in the fields during those years as an adolescent but also later earned a degree in agriculture and served for thirty years as a soil conservation officer for the United States Department of Agriculture. This is what he says about it:

> Until about the mid-thirties, [Southern] farming had not changed very much since the invention of the steel plow. Horses or mules were the main source of power; mules were the choice of Southern cotton farms while horses were used in the corn belt . . . Farming with mules was hard, slow work. A good team, in light soil, could pull a twelve-inch turning plow. Plowing an acre with this size plow required walking eight and one-fourth miles and at least a full day. It took a good mule to do this. Turning plows come in sizes from six to sixteen inches; the small ones were often used when cotton got very grassy to "sidebar" the cotton. This would leave a ridge

about four inches wide with the plants in the center. This ridge was hand chopped with a hoe to thin the cotton and remove the grass. An acre of cotton has about two and a quarter miles of rows; chopping an acre of cotton requires about 10,000 strokes of a hoe.

The work is not only hard but very monotonous. In a normal year, cotton was chopped at least twice and then it had to be "dirted." This consisted of going down each side of the row with a double shovel, a plow with two points on one shaft, and moving dirt back around the plants. This covered up any grass that had sprouted since chopping. If weather permitted, cotton was plowed about once per week until the plants shaded the middles. We always hoped for this to occur by 4 July, but it seldom happened this early.

. . . Daddy felt comfortable in familiar situations, which meant that he didn't especially like to make changes. But once he made a change, he didn't dwell on the past; he took off on a course to adapt to the change. I remember the first time a one-row cultivator came on the place. This was a simple machine that allowed one man to plow both sides of a row. This was about 1933 and was the beginning of the changes that displaced so many poor families in the South. It in effect did away with the need for one man. On that day, Daddy and Grover had gone to Dumas on Saturday afternoon in a Model A. Grover bought this cultivator and they towed it home behind the car. Daddy wasn't too happy, but it wasn't long before he got rid of all his double shovels. I think this cultivator cost eighty-five dollars, which was several bales of cotton at this time . . . We had a tractor before we had a cultivator. Grover bought a Fordson tractor for five dollars that ran on kerosene, had steel wheels and was cranked by hand. I could crank it with my right hand until it gave out and then switch to my left hand. Eventually it would start, though sometimes it would kick backwards and if you couldn't hold the crank, it would break your arm. This old tractor could only be used to pull a disc . . . About 1937 we got our first Farmall tractor. It had about eighteen horsepower, steel wheels, and burned tractor fuel. It had a small tank to hold gasoline to start it. After it got warm, we would switch over to the lower-priced tractor fuel. I think it cost eight cents per gallon

delivered. The electrical system was a magneto which pow-
ered the spark plugs. The magneto had a device on it to retard
the spark, otherwise it would kick like a mule when it was
cranked by hand. This tractor was about a 1929 model. We
bought a new five-and-a-half foot disc which was all it could
pull. It handled a two-row cultivator. This was lifted with three
levers, one for each front plow and one for the back gang. With
practice, you could lift the plows and turn without stopping.
We later got a mechanical lift for seventy-five dollars that
worked off the power take-off. This was a real advancement.[18]

Jodie does not mention in his description of the cotton-chop-
ping process that a working day traditionally went from dawn until
dark with an hour or an hour and a half off for the noon meal and
a short rest. Women who had to go home and fix the dinner left the
field at 11:30, and the mules were stopped and cared for then. The
rest of the workers went in at 12:00. A big "dinner bell" in our yard
was rung to mark the time at 11:30 and then again at 1:00. The
sound of that bell at any other time signified an emergency to which
everybody within hearing distance was expected to respond.

Harvesting cotton by hand was perhaps even harder than cultivating it with hoes: back-breaking stoop labor at its worst. There
were different sizes of cotton sacks. Made of heavy canvas with a
strap to go over the shoulder, these sacks were five feet long for small
children, seven feet long for lighter pickers like women and large
children and nine feet long for stronger workers. The picker pulled
the sack along between the rows and picked the cotton into it. Fast
pickers used both hands at lightning speed and picked two rows at
once. Slower pickers handled only one row at a time. By the time
cotton is ready to pick, the best is fluffy and hanging out of the dried
boll, which has cracked open to let it free. The worst is not fluffy or
hanging all the way out but is stuck so that the lint is protected by
the needle-sharp husk of the dried boll. It was up to the picker to
get as little trash like leaves and stems in it as possible. "Clean pickers" were treasured. When the picker's sack was full, it was weighed
and emptied into a wagon or a "cotton house," a little wooden house
on skids that could be pulled from field to field to hold the cotton

until it could be taken to the gin. Keeping it dry was crucial. Cotton houses were big enough to hold a bale of loose cotton, up to fifteen hundred pounds or so. (There are old photographs of cotton picking, like those by J. C. Coovert and George Francois Mugnier, with large baskets in evidence that have led some scholars to believe that cotton was sometimes picked into baskets. This was not true in our part of the Delta, and judging from the photographs themselves, I doubt that it was anywhere. The baskets were used to transport cotton from the sacks to the weighing station or to the waiting wagon. In the pictures in question, pickers are standing there with sack straps visible on their shoulders.)

"Weighing up" was usually done by a foreman or the landowner himself, and each picker's weights were carefully recorded and added up daily and weekly. Huddie Ledbetter, or "Leadbelly," the great African American folk singer, used to sing a song with a line that went, "I'm ona jump down turn around pick a bale o' cotton, jump down turn around, pick a bale a day," for urban white audiences who had no inkling of the unlikelihood of the accomplishment being bragged about. An un-ginned bale would weigh anywhere from 950 to 1500 pounds. Most pickers listed in Boss's daybook for 1941 picked fewer than 300 pounds a day; there was one, however, who picked 604 pounds in one day. The weights for each "weighing up" ranged from 38 to 66 pounds. The more information one gathers about handpicking cotton, the more impressive the task appears. For example, Donald Holley, in *The Second Great Emancipation,* gives the following data, "About 70 bolls made a pound of seed cotton, and a good day's work was considered to be 150 pounds. . . . If a picker gathered 150 pounds, which was usually the amount expected, he had to snatch about 10,500 bolls during a day. . . . It took 1500 pounds of seed cotton to make a 500 pound bale once the seeds were removed. A crop of 12 million bales demanded labor of about 4 million pickers over a period of forty workdays."[19]

Saturday was payday. Boss would go to town and draw cash for the payroll, and all the workers who could went along also to get paid where they could spend their hard-earned money and visit with friends they saw only on Saturday afternoons. Dumas on Saturday in those days was like a festival. The main street of town, with the railroad splitting it down the middle, was absolutely jammed with people strolling and visiting and window shopping. Many threw their money away or lost it in crap games every Saturday. Considering how hard they had to work to earn it, it is hard to blame them for relishing the momentary pleasure. The jail filled up on Saturdays, and landowners would have to bail out their tenants on Sunday if they were to be at work on Monday. Fines were listed as loans in the accounts and deducted from the tenant's share at settling-up time in the fall.

In spite of the back-breaking labor, there was a camaraderie among the cotton pickers that I, a small child with nobody to play with, envied. They worked along the rows in a group; the faster pickers working two rows at a time did not often outpace the slower ones working only one row. Most of them had known each other all their lives as had their parents and grandparents before them. Most were black, but by the mid-1930s, there were large numbers of white tenant farmers who had come down from the mountain counties northwest of Little Rock because the soil on their hill farms wore out as the Depression and drought hit and they could no longer make a living. White and black together out there in those fields were in one boat for a while, and they talked as they worked. It seemed to me that the field workers had a much better time than anybody in my family ever had, and I begged constantly to be allowed to go too. One Saturday when I was about ten, this was permitted. I was fitted out with a straw hat and a small sack and sent to the field early in the morning with the crew. Within two hours I was exhausted and would have been left behind if the others hadn't picked from my row—into my sack, of course—because they were kind people and did not want me to feel bad about my incompetence. At noon when I got to the house, I sank to the floor in the living room, too tired to eat, and fell sound asleep. Once was enough. I never went back again, and from that morning I understood, first of all, why people who did not have to did not work in the fields and, second, that it was terrible for the ones who were forced to do it. My experience in the field must have taken place about 1941. The payment for picking that year was a penny a pound. So George Jenkins, the man who did the gargantuan feat of picking 604 pounds made $6.04 that day; most of the others, for the same amount of time, earned less than half that much!

The boll weevil, which arrived in our part of the world about 1918, had become a raging problem by the 1930s. Most of the weevil damage is caused by the females' laying eggs in the cotton squares, the pre-bloom buds. Adults also puncture squares and eat their contents. Either way, the damaged square is killed and falls off. The cycle from egg to adult takes only three weeks, so five or more generations per year is not unusual. The accepted treatment in the 1930s and '40s was to dust with lead arsenic. Jodie recalls that machines to apply the poison were expensive, so farmers improvised. A common applicator consisted of two twenty-four-pound flour sacks tied on each end of a five foot pole. A man on a mule rode up and down between the rows bouncing this pole on the mule's back and shaking poison on the cotton. This was done at night so the dew would hold the dust on the leaves. The mule wore a muzzle to keep him from eating poisoned cotton; the man had to fare for himself. It has only been in the last few years that a concerted, coordinated effort to control the boll weevil has been successful. Billions of dollars have been lost, and for the individual farmer dealing with them, they have posed a problem as serious as the weather.

The Great Depression, the second ingredient in the crucible that refined the family's fortunes, arrived while they were still reeling from the Flood, and the decade from 1930 to 1940 might be compared to a long siege with a life-threatening disease that would either kill the patients or leave them forever altered from whatever they had been before they got it. (One of the lasting results was a carefulness with money that is hard for subsequent generations to comprehend.) In addition to the Depression, the greatest drought to ever hit the South and Southwest occurred in 1930. While many farmers found it impossible to make enough corn to feed their mules, Jodie recalls that then and in subsequent droughts our farm was able to make enough corn to at least feed the animals.

By the end of 1937, however, things looked better for the farm. They had paid the delinquent taxes and taken possession of Round

Brake by the end of March that year; they were optimistic enough about the future to make plans for six new tenant houses; and they even bought a new pickup truck, a bright red Dodge with a leaping ram as a hood ornament. Furthermore, the effects of the New Deal were tangible in the form of cash payments for participation in the crop allotment programs.

There is no question that from its inception in 1933 until 2004, the last year any of us did row-crop farming on this place, the New Deal with its evolving programs provided an essential factor in enabling this family to hang onto its land. The primary source of assistance to Boss and Grover was the AAA, the Agricultural Adjustment Administration, which instituted a plan to raise the price of cotton by limiting production. To begin, producers were given cash for plowing up a portion of their cotton crop. This land could then be used for cultivation of soil-improvement crops not sold on the open market or for food and feed crops for home use. Jodie remembers that in 1933, the first year that payments were offered in exchange for plowing up cotton, Boss received $30 per acre for plowing up one third of his crop, eleven acres. This $330 was enough cash to pay the costs of the other two-thirds. Jodie does not remember exactly how the payments were divided with the tenants but is certain that they were; he thinks the tenants' shares were applied against their "furnish" debt rather than given as a cash payment. He recalls that Boss was scrupulous in giving his tenants every penny due them. Another benefit of the subsidy program was a job for the twenty-one-year-old Grover surveying croplands for AAA to certify the acreage involved in the programs. When Jodie got old enough, he did the same. That first trickle of government subsidy turned into a steady stream and finally into a roaring river that paid Casey, Grover's son, $600,000 between 1998 and 2003.[20]

There were other helpful programs also; Zena, my mother, attended monthly meetings of the local women's home demonstration club run by the agricultural extension service, where she learned such practical things as methods of food preservation and how to make new mattresses out of raw cotton and striped bed ticking. She actually made some mattresses that were as tight and neat and comfortable as store-bought ones. These meetings were her only social occasions, aside from church and family and visits with her close friend Roberta Irby, and she enjoyed them tremendously. I remember one she hosted at our house to which thirty or forty women, including the county home demonstration agent, came bringing a pot-luck lunch of fantastic food. A business meeting followed lunch, and then a demonstration was given of some process that I have forgotten. When the meeting was adjourned, everyone went out to admire the flowers and be given seeds and cuttings from shrubs if they wanted them. I suspect this ritual with the garden was the one most enjoyed by all.

Another government program beneficial to us was the 4-H program administered by the county agents. Bob had a project raising purebred Duroc Jersey hogs, and I raised chickens for mine. The 4-H program is an ingenious way of teaching future farmers the value of investing in quality stock and managing money. The Merchants and Farmers' Bank in Dumas loaned Bob twenty dollars to buy a purebred Duroc Jersey sow, registered as "Dumas Lady Bob" but called "Susie" by us, of which we were inordinately proud. As pigs go, she was beautiful, a Miss America among swine. He was to repay the bank when he sold her pigs, and then the rest of the profits from the sale would be his. I think Boss financed my venture, which was to order a batch of Rhode Island Red baby chicks from Sears, Roebuck and raise them for eggs to sell. When World War II began, hogs and eggs were suddenly worth cash—enough to repay Bob's loan and buy a pony for him, a bicycle for me, and countless $25 war bonds after that. I still remember the exhilaration of earning that first money. I was ten years old and selling twenty dozen eggs a week for the unheard-of sum of twenty cents a dozen!

In the unceasing fight against poverty that the Depression was for us, there were other mitigating circumstances than the unexpected gift of Round Brake that made things easier. For example, by 1933 the government was ready to make the death payments promised to the families of soldiers killed on duty in World War I. Zena's brother, William Cason, had been killed in France, and the payment to the family was split equally among his remaining siblings and the two orphaned children of his brother and sister who had died. So Zena received her portion of three hundred dollars as well as that of Ted Willis, the nephew she and Boss had taken in at birth. This sum was enough to encourage her to press her suit for a new house to replace the old one that had been flooded in 1927 and still smelled so strongly of mold that she was sure it would never be fresh again. Zena was a soft-spoken woman who hated confrontation, but in this she persisted in the face of strong opposition from Boss and Sallie who loved their childhood home and did not want it torn down. She had an answer to all their objections and was obstinate in her insistence. For once she would not budge. The new house, built by Boss and Grover on the exact spot where the old one had stood and incorporating many salvaged materials from that house, had more space, including five bedrooms, and, best of all, had the kitchen inside it. No longer would Zena have to go across a breezeway in all weather to the outside kitchen to cook breakfast. Building this house seems to have given the family courage and, I am certain, pride. It is easy to imagine the speculation in the countryside about how, at a time when others were losing their homes and farms, the Joneses were building a new house!

It must be mentioned that another major mitigating factor during those cashless years was Zena's personality. With a will of iron and an optimistic outlook that would not entertain the notion of failure she admonished us daily to pull up our socks and keep them up. Her most often repeated mottos were, "Do the best you can with what you have," and, "Look on the bright side." As she did. She believed in the power of parables, and the one I recall most vividly, because it was so frightening to me as a child, involved a man so lazy that his community decided to bury him alive because he would not work and take care of his family. As they were taking him to the graveyard in a coffin, one of the pallbearers said he could not bear to do this terrible thing and would donate a bushel of corn for him to start over with. The lazy man sat up and asked, "Is it shelled?" and when told that it was not, lay down again and said, "If it ain't shelled, walk on, boys. You might as well go on and bury me."

Daughter of a Methodist minister and steeped in unquestioning faith, Zena drew great comfort from her absolute belief that our

fortunes were part of a divine plan, especially during the worst financial times and while my brothers were away at war. Another favorite
saying of hers was, "Things work out for the best for those who love
the Lord." And we were taken to Sunday school and church every
Sunday morning to have this view affirmed by a preacher and con-
gregation. There was never any question about whether anyone in
the family was going to church. Everyone not too ill to walk went.

Zena raised our food in her garden and poultry yard and made
our clothes so well that we went to school and church better dressed
than most and with our heads up because she had instructed us,
"Remember who you are and set a good example." Another financial contribution she made to the family income lay in her enterprise
in boarding a Watson schoolteacher from the autumn of 1938 until
1942. This teacher, Miss Mary Myrtle Jones (no relation), was like a
member of the family, and the paltry sum charged for her room and
board was useful beyond belief.

Although things were looking better by 1938, when the family
bought the Bodine Place, still no one slept easy. There was always
the threat of any of a number of possible disasters like drought, the
inability to control insects, or another failure of the economic system that could dry up credit and cause us to have to mortgage the
land for furnish money—and then lose it. It happened all around
us: itinerant cotton pickers who only a year before had owned their
own places turned up every fall seeking work. And there was never
any question in anyone's mind that our welfare depended on owning the land.

By 1942, however, the farm's situation was beginning to ease,
for World War II brought prosperity. According to the IRS form
1065 filed in 1943, the partnership of G. C. Jones & Son earned a
gross income of $9,565.99 in 1942 and after deductions showed a
net income of $4,632.81 to be divided between Boss and Grover.
That year they sold $7,063.34 worth of cotton, $1,404 worth of cotton seed, $60 worth of livestock, and $200 worth of other seed,
probably oats; they also received $340 from "governmental rental."
On the deduction schedule they listed as depreciable assets 1 tractor and combine, 1 truck, 7 houses, 3 barns, 8 mules, and 2 horses.[21]

A corner had been turned, and in spite of a few lean years in the 1950s, the farm has never been in dire financial straits again.

Boss's ledgers show him to have been a meticulous record keeper. Jodie remembers that when the farm began to make money in the early years of World War II, the IRS asked Boss to let them use his books as a benchmark against which to evaluate the tax returns of neighbors who were still not claiming profits.

The accounts for the G. C. Jones & Son operation that are available for the years 1949–1956 contain a wealth of information. In his ledgers, Boss kept three disbursement accounts: one for the partnership, where he itemized all expenses except for loans to the tenants; another for loans to individual tenants, including "furnish" money and the cost of day labor needed to make their crops; and a third account listing each bale of cotton sold with the weight of lint and seed and the name of the owner, either a tenant or the partnership. These figures make possible a close approximation of their income from cotton and the cost of producing it. It was the major cash crop each year, although they may have sold a few cows and some corn as well.

In addition to these business accounts, Boss kept a careful account listing the expenses of the household, so we can see how he spent his money. The household was still shared by Grover, a bachelor living at home but with a room in Arkansas City, the county seat, where he stayed when official business kept him in that part of the county. Pauline and Jodie were both married and living in Watson; Ted was at the University of Arkansas at Fayetteville, on the GI Bill; Bob was at Mississippi State, also on the GI Bill; and I was at Hendrix College, a small private Methodist college in Conway, Arkansas. It was a banner year for cotton in 1948, and Boss had been able to put aside enough money for four years of my college expenses, so those do not appear in his accounts.

Before looking at the ledgers for 1949, one hundred years into the family's ownership of the farm, an explanation of the system of tenant farming may be useful. It is, after all, this system, and its predecessor, slavery, that distinguishes this model of the American family farm from those in other regions of the country. Basically, the arrange-

ments are that landowner and tenant agree on the amount of land the
tenant will work. There are two types of tenants: renters and sharecroppers. Renters, who retain three-quarters of the cotton and two-
thirds of the corn, provide their own tools, stock, equipment, and
financial resources. In other words, they rent the land and sometimes
a house on it for payment of a portion of their production.
Sharecroppers get half the cotton and a quarter of the corn raised on
their allotments; the landowner gets the rest. In 1949, as in most other
years, Boss and Grover's tenants were sharecroppers, not renters, and
did not raise corn, so the proceeds of the cotton, their only crop, were
split equally between owner and tenant. The landowner was obliged
to provide a livable house, tilling equipment of either mules and plows
or tractors and implements, a garden spot, and tools such as hoes (but
not cotton sacks), and Boss provided pasturage for cows if anyone had
them. There was also, and foremost in the agreement with sharecroppers, "furnish," a loan of money for food, clothing, medical care, fines,
etc., from March 1 until September 1. By then the tenants could
expect to earn enough in the fields and from the sale of their crops
to feed themselves until March 1 of the following year. The tenants,
in turn, were obliged to provide the labor required to make the crop
on their allotted pieces of ground. It was expected that the work
would be done properly and in a timely fashion. If the labor provided
by their own families was inadequate, others were called in to help
and were paid out of the tenant's share of the gross income.

The farming year really began on March 1, "Furnish Day," when
the landowner would borrow enough money from a bank, or other
lender such as a gin owner, to support all of his tenants until
September 1. It took careful negotiation and a collateral mortgage on
everything on the place except the land itself to get this sum. Before
going to the bank, the landlord would have already made his arrangements with the tenants as to how much land each would get to work,
depending on the number of workers in the family and the subsequent amount each could draw monthly to live on, for nobody could
expect to draw more than could be repaid from the tenant's half of
the crop. Since the landowner was paying interest to the bank on this
loan, the tenants paid interest on the amounts they received. When

the cotton was sold, the landowner and tenant went over the accounts, gin tickets, and sales slips to determine the gross receipts and the amount the tenant would receive. From the tenant's half, the landowner subtracted the amount that had been drawn as "furnish" and other loans as well as any amount owed from the previous year, and then handed over the remainder, if any, to the tenant. Out of the other half, which he kept, he had to pay the expenses of maintenance on the tenant houses, the costs of equipment, mules, tractors, implements, hauling cotton to the gin, feed, and everything else required to make the crop. But first, he had to repay the bank. A few bad years in a row could put him on the road to California as a migrant worker or in a neighbor's field as a tenant farmer.

In addition to the tenants' crops, most landowners, including Boss and Grover, had a "day crop" of their own, which was worked by the tenants for cash. This "day crop," which included corn, lespedeza, oats, and sometimes sorghum as well as cotton, gave the tenants another source of income, as their own crops did not require all of their working time, and they were paid cash when called on to help. Of course, the day crop gave the owners a source of income as well, and it is worth noting that in Boss's accounts, the wages paid white and black laborers were exactly the same: forty cents per hour, in 1949. It is also worth noting that it was my father's pride that when he settled with the tenants, the gin tickets for the cotton sold reflected the real amount he had received for it. He did not keep a double set of books to cheat them with; some gin owners were perfectly willing to provide two sets of tickets for this very purpose.

In 1949, the farm produced 102 bales of cotton, and if they received the average price of 28.7¢ per pound for it, their gross was $14,842. They also received $542 for cotton seed. The tenants' share was $6,959, of which $5,681 was owed and repaid by them to the partnership for furnish and other loans. (One of the tenants refused to work his cotton properly and, rather than doing it the required way, left in the middle of the night, abandoning both crop and debts.) The farm's expenses, including the $750 payment on the Bodine Place, amounted to $8,053. After paying the bank what they owed on the "furnish" loan, $6,678, Boss and Grover were left with

$6,354 to split equally between them. Since their single-entry book-keeping listed only outlays, there is no accounting of receipt of their government subsidy payments, which undoubtedly went directly into the bank account when received and were used to pay expenses like ordinary income.

The household expenditures give a notion of the kind of life this income of $3,177 afforded. First of all, it should be noted that some food was still raised on the place: there is an order for a payment for fifty baby chickens and feed, so eggs and chickens for the family's consumption were still provided in the yard. A hog was bought, but rather than slaughtering and curing the meat themselves as they once would have done, meat processing and curing at a storage freezer in Dumas were paid for. I don't believe that Mother still had a large garden, but she may have had a few tomato plants. The house was now heated with butane gas; there was a gas cookstove and electricity, which also provided a pump for running water. They had no rent or mortgage payment on the house to pay.

In the household accounts, there are small disbursements of pocket money to Bob and me. Subscriptions were paid to *Life* magazine and *Reader's Digest* as well as *The Arkansas Gazette* and *The McGehee Times,* the state and county papers we read. Since Mother, who had made our clothes for years, was in poor health by that time, most of her clothes and mine were ordered from two department stores in Little Rock, Gus Blass and Pfeifer's; the payments are duly recorded as are all the grocery and gasoline bills. My father was absolutely even-handed in patronizing the local businesses. There was a store a mile or so on each side of the farm, and he alternated buying gas and groceries between them. There were two hardware stores in Dumas owned by brothers who did not speak to each other. Boss alternated his purchases between them. Every time.

The accounts of the household's basic expenses for three adults and the vacation visits of two college students show how far money went in 1949. That year they paid $486.62 for groceries, $61.60 for electricity, $131.98 for butane gas, $75.95 for prescription drugs, and $17.00 in doctor bills.

There is one extraordinary purchase that tells how prosperous my father was beginning to feel. For Zena's birthday he ordered a cameo from M. W. Goldsmith, a jeweler in Memphis, and paid $320 for it! That was a lot of money in 1949, and this is the only time I can remember his ever buying anything like that for her. My mother was extremely reclusive, by that time, and aside from church went nowhere at all; from then on she wore that cameo on Sundays for the rest of her life.

As for what our life was like, people I have told this story to over the years have had difficulty understanding the isolation in which we lived—that there could have been so little in the way of entertainment and social life. For one thing, the South at that time was almost feudal in its social structure, and for a long time there were no other families in the immediate vicinity to visit with. Also, my mother's reclusive nature had a lot to do with our isolation; the Irby family lived about three miles away, and Mrs. Irby was my mother's only close friend for many years. While Mrs. Irby was alive, we saw a great deal of that family, there being children near the same age in both households. But she died before the beginning of World War II, and there was no one else after that for my mother and, consequently, for the rest of us.

Going to a "picture show" meant driving twenty-four miles over a gravel road there and back. Boss refused to go to movies, for some reason, once sound tracks were introduced, and Mother did not drive. When Miss Jones, the teacher who boarded with us, was there, occasionally she and Mother and I would go on a Sunday afternoon, but she left about 1942. Church on Sunday was about all the social activity there was, and in addition to its religious significance, it meant a great deal to my family as a place to see other people. (There was a joke in our house about it: we were like a woman who had worked for the family at some point who replied, when asked why she went to church, "I goes to see and be saw.") In Joseph's time, the family attended a Methodist church, served by a circuit rider, two miles away, on the road to the Irby place, but sometime in Boss's tenure that church closed, and the family began attending the Methodist church in Watson. When Grover came home from the war, he switched to the Methodist church in Dumas, and I went with him, as I was going to school in Dumas, by that time, and all my friends were there.

My chief entertainment was riding a horse. My friend Betsy Ross lived three miles away, and in the difficult adolescent years when my own family bored me to death, I spent every possible minute at her house. As long as I went on the horse and did not have to be carried and fetched, my family did not care how long I stayed, which suited me fine. She had a horse also, and we rode together through the fields to the levee or to a lake a few miles away. Betsy was three years older than I and was as determined to go away and see the world as I was. Our conversations and the leisure we had to engage in them were my greatest pleasures in those days and a shaping influence on my life. Her family became as important to me as my own, and I named my first son after her father. Betsy earned a Ph.D. also and, after her children were grown, had a career as an officer in the foreign service that took her to Europe, Africa, and the Middle East. It must say something about the prevailing culture that few people can imagine that, within a ten mile radius of our farmhouse, in my generation, there are three Ph.D.'s, an M.D., four engineers, numerous Bachelors of Science in agriculture, and several teachers—and this in a part of the South that the rest of the country has been at pains to tell me was the deepest pit of ignorance in the United States! With little else to do, people read, and read, and read, and then went to see. The GI Bill helped, of course, as it enabled many veterans to attend college who otherwise might not have been able to do so, but it is worth noting that our high schools were adequate to prepare students for college work.

Another factor that should not be overlooked was the attitude in our house and the Irby house, and in others as well, that education was valuable and that the teachers who provided it should be respected. Moreover, while it is tempting to think only of the cultural deprivation inherent in that isolation, it must be remembered that when Uriah came to the frontier, he brought his library. So from the beginning, there were expectations that ideas coming from outside our experience were desirable. And there was also, from the beginning, a belief that good manners would enable us to go anywhere and do anything. These beliefs went with the territory of that culture, and I have not doubted them to this day.

I should mention that our house did not have a telephone until about 1954. I considered this a crippling detriment to my social life when I was in high school, but even after the service was available, sometime in the 1940s my father flatly refused to have one in the house. He said once the boys were home from the War, there was nobody outside that house he wanted to talk to, so we did not need one. After Zena's death, when Pauline moved out there with her family to take care of him, she insisted on having a telephone.

Since I went into great detail about our life in *Born in the Delta,* I will not go into it in detail here except to say that it was lonely and dull, more interesting to the men and boys who were actually engaged in the farming operation than to the women and girls more or less confined to the house and yard. I have often pondered whether I might have liked to be a cotton farmer, had I been a boy. It certainly had its appeal, but I think the truth is that for Jodie, Ted, Bob, and me, leaving there for a different kind of life was a goal from childhood.

So if this was the life we got from the living made during the tenant-farming phase of the farm's history, what was it like on the other side of the equation, that of the tenant farmers who did the work? In 1949 the partnership had four black and five white share-croppers. The accounts for one of the black tenants, Jim Figures and his family, can be taken as an example to illustrate the situation of the sharecropper. Jim Figures began the year 1949 with a debt of $17.21 carried over from 1948 and ended it with a debt of $180.76 to be carried over to 1950. It was the story of his and many other sharecrop-pers' lives and was due not to lack of diligence on his part nor to avaricious, heartless, mean slave-driving on the part of the landowner but to the nature of the system itself, which nobody ever defended, as far as I know. Jim and his family were hard workers. Boss was hon-est and compassionate in his dealings with them, but it was simply not possible for that family to provide enough labor to make a profit in this system.

Jim drew $1,477.28 including $635 and other loans in furnish and $634.64 for labor to help with his crop. He made eighteen bales of cotton for a total weight of 9,035 pounds, which if sold at the aver-age price of 28.7¢ per pound, brought $2,593. Half went to the part-nership and half ($1,296.52) to Jim, but he owed $1,477.28 to the partnership. He also earned $130.10 for labor for Boss and others on the farm, probably the only money he earned aside from his crop. Although he had a large family, most of them were children too small to be much help in the field; he was furnished only five nine-foot sacks that year, so his labor force must have consisted of two adults and three large children. Jim's wife Victory's wages for doing our laundry do not show up in the accounts. She was paid in cash, surely at a lesser rate than the 40¢ an hour paid field hands, so her contribution would have been small. It was simply not possible for them to earn more money.

Nobody would deny that sharecroppers had a hard life. The houses thought adequate for them were poorly built, two- or three-room shotgun houses with cracks around the doors and windows that let the wind whistle through; heat was provided by a wood stove, and water came from a pump in the yard. (The rooms in a "shotgun" house are in a straight line so that a shot fired through the front door would go straight through the entire house, killing everybody in it—hence the name, according to legend.) The schools for black children had short terms to allow time for working in the fields. White tenants' children who went to school during the harvest season were expected to grab their cotton sacks or hoes and head to the field the minute they stepped off the bus. And yet, in spite of hardship, many of the children of those families went on to do well at other things. The sons in one African American family, headed by a remarkable woman named Queen Rainey, did well indeed. One, David Rainey, became a high school teacher, then assistant principal of the prestigious Arkansas School for Mathematics, Sciences and the Arts in Hot Springs, and later a state legislator. Another, Joe Jones, married Jim and Victory's oldest daughter Easter Mae and became one of Grover's tractor drivers and then his right-hand man at the Pendleton gin. Easter Mae went on to become a clerk at a department store in Dumas. Toy Thomas, Bob's age and son of a tenant farmer, married and had twelve children, eleven of whom have college degrees.

Our relations with the tenants varied with the individuals. Several black families were associated with the farm and family over several generations. The McDonald, Hicks, and Jackson families are listed as close neighbors in the census records from 1880 forward. I cannot account for their absence from the 1870 census, as they were said to have been slaves belonging to Uriah Jones, or Ira E. Brown, and so should have been listed in the census. They lived on the land near Uriah's house, which Aunt Maggie and Uncle Henry Saine lost in 1929, and after that moved a mile or so away.

"Aunt" Amanda Hicks was the Jones cook when Mother went there to board in 1908. Jim Figures, whom I have already mentioned, was the grandson of John McDonald, who married Victoria Bowen and lived on the place until 1966. When the days of sharecropping were over as Grover mechanized the place in the 1950s and '60s, Jim remained as a tractor driver. These were people we cared about—Jim's wife Victory worked for us in the house when she was not needed in the fields, and the memory of my conversations with her are as important to me as any others from my formative years. As she washed and ironed, we talked, and each of us listened to the other more carefully than I suspect anyone else listened to either of us. She did not laugh at my dreams, and I did not take lightly the difficulties of her life. There were long, close personal ties between our families, and during my father's final illness he extracted a promise from Grover that they would have a home on the place as long as they wanted it, a promise that Grover kept until they left for Chicago to join some of their children in 1966. The ties with this family continued into the next generation as their son-in-law Joe Jones worked with Grover for over thirty years. Grover left instructions that Joe be asked to be a pallbearer at his funeral.

Another tenant, who came to be like a member of our family, was a white man named Clyo Moore. In about 1930 Clyo, who was about sixteen, and his brother J. D., who was about fourteen, had differences with their stepfather, a tenant on what had been Aunt Maggie's land, and needed a place to stay. The second floor of our house was a dormitory for boys; my brothers slept up there as well as cousins who came every summer to stay a few weeks or months and do whatever the brothers were doing. So Mother put the Moore brothers up there with them. Six boys were not much more trouble than four, and their willing help on the farm was appreciated. J. D.

joined the navy when he finished high school and eventually retired as a lieutenant commander. Clyo stayed until he married a wonderful woman named Wilma and then moved with her to a tenant house on the place where they remained until their seventies, except for a few years after his stepfather's death when he farmed his mother's land. When Grover mechanized, Clyo became his foreman and drove a tractor as well.

They were there at least sixty years and in Mother's final years looked after her as if she had been their own mother. That one time I was allowed to go to the field to pick cotton was only because Wilma took me with her. Clyo, like a member of the family in many respects, was the man called upon to direct the digging of graves in the family cemetery when any of us died. He knew exactly where the old graves, some unmarked, were and where the next one should go, according to family and generation. He and Wilma could have been buried there as well but chose the cemetery in Dumas instead, near his mother's grave.

In addition to this stable contingent of people who stayed for years, there was a continually shifting population of tenants that we did not know as well. Through the '30s the number of white families grew as more and more people became displaced because of the Depression and because of the progressive depletion of the soil in the mountainous areas of Arkansas. Some stayed for a few years and then were able to buy land of their own, with assistance from the government and their own hard work. Others moved on to California. Bob and Jodie can list twenty-six families, black and white, that they recall living on the place between 1927 and 1966.

I would not presume to try to tell the tenant farmers' story because I do not know enough about it. But they are beginning to tell it themselves. For example, Janis Kearney, Bill Clinton's private diarist during his White House years, has written an eloquent account of life in an African American tenant family's household, some fifteen miles from our farm, called *Cotton Field of Dreams*. And the legendary white rockabilly and blues singer Billy Lee Riley, who grew up in a sharecropping family a hundred miles north of us, near Forest City, and began working in the fields at ten, gave a graphic description in an interview of the difficult nature of the work and the deprivation suffered by his family that included the following interesting revelation:

> It's something I wouldn't want to see my children have to do, but I wouldn't mind having to do it again . . . that was such a good time for me. And I'm constantly comparing life today and life back then . . . Back then, nobody had anything; there were only two classes. The ones that had everything and those that didn't have anything. And it didn't bother us. We didn't care. The people we knew didn't have any more than we did so we thought that's the way everybody lived. People loved each other. You could go to a neighbor's house and if they had any-thing they'd give it to you. They wouldn't expect it back . . . If we were hungry and a neighbor had food, nine times out of ten we didn't have to ask for it. They would bring it and share it. And that's what I miss. I miss the love between neighbors.[22]

It is tempting for those looking on from outside to view the lives of tenant families as a constant struggle in unmitigated misery because of our inability from our perspective to know of the pleas-ures and rewards that made life tolerable. For example, again, Riley recalls the pleasure that went with it as well as the pain. This is a seventy-year-old man recalling following a plow as a child:

> The first thing I remember about it was the aroma, a very nice aroma, you following mules all day. But it was beautiful. The smell of that land, that new land turning over was great. But what it was, we would first take what you would call a turning plow, a plow pulled by two mules, and you would take one row at a time. It would actually turn the dirt upside down. And my brother would be following me doing the same thing, or he would be in front and we would do this, we had twenty-five acres of cotton land, and it just took forever to do it. We would spend ten or twelve hours a day doing it. Then we would take this little riding disc, and we had only one of them and we would fight over who was going to get to ride, then we would go over the land with that, and we would take a har-row and smooth it all off, get the clods out, then we had what

you call a two-row hopper, and it had a little seat and it had little hoppers filled with cotton seed, and one guy would be planting while the other would be waiting on the end to fill up those hoppers, and then we would put fertilizer down the same way. And then we would wait for cotton to sprout and when it got about two inches high we would get out there and chop it and then the cotton would grow. We would chop it twice while it was growing and a third time when it was about two feet high . . . and then you would run the middles with this cultivator we'd been using to plow the cotton. After we'd run the middles, farming was over until harvest time. So it was a big job.[23]

The best way I can think of to describe our lives and those of the people around us in those days is to think of our inhabiting different spheres that behaved like bubbles. There were spheres for landowners, black tenants, white tenants, et cetera, that coexisted sometimes as discrete entities and sometimes merged for periods of time, and there were characteristic modes of behavior for each with certain levels of respect expected for all. It was the function of manners to negotiate transactions between the inhabitants of all the spheres according to certain codes; there was trouble when these codes were violated. The social landscape, including race relations and relations between landed and landless whites, was a minefield too complicated to go into here as fully as it deserves. It was a hierarchical, racist society, and our family was as involved in these societal expectations as it was in all the others. We were snobs where "common" people were concerned, and while we were taught to treat black people with respect, we were also taught that they were, simply, "other," different and less than we.

The society was unrelenting in this acculturation, which was, after all, backed by law. As children we knew better, and some of us held on to this knowledge and agonized over our participation in wrongs exacted by the culture. And for the most part, we left. I was gone for sixteen years and returned in 1968 to a place not socially integrated—the churches and country clubs and honkytonks were as segregated as they had ever been—but the schools were integrated, and there were black public officials and law enforcement officers all over the state, especially in the Delta.

It is interesting to me that when laws for integrating the public schools were enacted, the schools in Watson and Dumas were integrated without a hitch. The riots and bloodbaths that had always been predicted did not happen there. A small "Seg" academy was organized in Gould, a few miles north of Dumas, but it did not prosper. In the 1950s there were white men in my father's generation who would not watch sports events on television that included black athletes. After school integration, before anybody seemed to notice, the mainstays of high school football and basketball teams were black, and everybody cheered. There was a glitch in McGehee, twenty miles from the farm, the first year a black student was elected football queen. The school board balked, saying it would cancel the festivities and that McGehee was not ready for such a step. The matter was settled when the mothers of the black players on the team announced that their sons would not play unless the team's choice was accepted. The queen was crowned, the players played, and that was it.

World War II brought deep emotional strain to Boss and Zena, for before it was over, all four sons and their son-in-law, William Lloyd, were called into service in the armed forces. Jodie, the first to go, was called up with his national guard unit from college and sent to the Aleutians, Grover and Ted served in the air force in Europe, and Bob served in the navy in the South Pacific, as did Bill Lloyd in the marines. All returned without a scratch. Jodie, Ted, and Bob finished college on the GI Bill and went on to seek their fortunes elsewhere, Bill Lloyd went into business with his father in a welding shop in Watson, and Grover returned to run the farm in partnership with Boss, among other things, for he, as had the farmers before him in the family, looked for outside income, in his case through politics.

Like many returning GIs, Grover came home from the war with political ambitions and ran for the office of tax assessor in 1946, counting on the support of returning servicemen. One campaign poster that brought him a certain amount of razzing had a picture of him standing in front of the Brandenburg Gate in Berlin with a confident smile on his face, legs wide apart, hands behind his back, and his cap on straight. The implication was that Sergeant Jones, who had saved the world from tyranny, was now prepared for whatever the citizens of Desha County could throw at him. He was elected and served for twenty years, voluntarily stepping aside in 1966 to devote himself to the farm and to run the Pendleton gin for the cooperative Pendleton Ginning Association at nearby Back Gate.

It had long been thought that although the land in Arkansas County, directly across the Arkansas River, was ideally suited for raising rice, the land on our side, the south side, was not, that it was too porous to hold water for the necessary flooding of the fields. But after World War II, this was found not to be true, and farmers in Desha County began to raise rice with success. So, in 1951, after a great deal of discussion in which Grover finally prevailed, the partners decided to try rice farming. This was a big decision for them because, in the first place, it meant sacrificing the idea that cotton would continue to be the farm's major cash crop, an especially disturbing idea for Boss, for whom raising cotton was what farming was all about. In the second place, setting up for rice was an expensive proposition. In 1949, their total expenses amounted to $7,739; in 1951, they laid out $4,712 of borrowed money for the rice operation alone, to pay for the irrigation pump, ditching, seed, and electricity. Moreover, they planted it on eighty acres of very good land, the last to be cleared, in fact, on the Bodine Place. Since rice is not as labor intensive as cotton , it also meant letting some of the tenants go. That year the farm was down to five tenant families.[24]

Jodie recalls that when Boss saw the mess the rice tractors made in the fields harvesting rice, he was ready to quit right then, their very first year. Bob remembers that the return on rice in 1951 was disappointing. The plants looked good but did not produce well. The problem was one shared by many other new rice producers and stemmed from the fact that rice would not produce well on land that had been previously planted in cotton that was poisoned with arsenic. Nobody, including the county agent, knew what to do. What they did was plant it again and again for three or four years and then go back to cotton because the results on that particular piece of ground continued to be disappointing. Later, when the problem had been diagnosed, they planted rice successfully on other land, but the expensive pump stood reproachfully idle for years in the middle of a large field, with crops growing around it, until finally it was used to irrigate cotton and paid for itself many times over.

In 1951, they ginned sixty-six bales of cotton. There are no figures in the ledger for the rice production, but the rice venture had major implications for the way the farm would go in the future, for the number of tenant families dropped to three in 1952 and they began to raise more hay, oats, and cattle. By then, only one pair of mules was kept for pulling corn; there were two saddle horses, one for my father to look at—he never rode anymore—and one for me, in case I ever came home again and wanted to ride. (In September 1952, I left for graduate school in St. Louis and never lived there again, although that farm is obviously still very much the center of my imagination.)

In 1954, with only three tenant farmers remaining, Boss and Grover began hiring more outside machine labor, depending on neighbors to do the disking, fertilizing, and hay baling. They were also building new fences with discarded railroad ties for posts, a sign that raising cattle was to be taken more seriously. They ginned seventy-eight bales of cotton that year, the only crop on which they kept complete records in the ledger, in addition to rice, oats, lespedeza hay, and cattle. Each partner took a $2,500 profit at the end of the year.

By 1950, Boss and Zena had a measure of prosperity and an empty nest in which to enjoy it. He bought a new car that he jokingly referred to as "Zee's automobile," as everyone knew that she did not drive, and instead of being lonely as the children had predicted, they got along quite well without us, in spite of her declining health. They had, after all, had children in the public schools for twenty-six years and still had one in college, but it must have been a tremendous relief to have most of the responsibility off their shoulders.

Zena died on December 7, 1953, and Pauline, with her husband Bill Lloyd and their children Sue and Billy, moved out to the farm to live in the house with Boss and take care of him. He was in poor health by then and seemed to take pleasure in little besides his grandson Billy whom he had had little chance to get to know before.

Boss died on December 26, 1957. He had been in charge of the farm fifty-one of his seventy-one years and had nursed it from an impending disaster to a thriving enterprise. He was buried next to Zena in the family cemetery with his parents and siblings and two of his children. As I have already mentioned, the cemetery was again in the family's hands.

CHAPTER 5

The Grover Generation

1957–1991

When Grover became sole manager of the farm, he was forty-five years old and had the experience of some thirty years of farming behind him. There was no question that he would take over at our father's death and run the place, as he had been doing so much of the management for years. In his will, Boss left each of his six children forty acres. Pauline was to have the house and forty acres it sat on, and rightly so. She had sacrificed her own home in Watson to move out to the farm with her husband and two children to take care of Boss and Grover when Zena died in 1953. Since Grover already owned 160 acres of the Bodine Place, he now had two hundred of his own and farmed the remainder for the rest of us. However, within a few years, Jodie, Ted, and Bob sold their portions to him, and I sold mine to Pauline. He continued to rent Pauline's eighty acres, as did his son Casey when he succeeded him as manager.

The farm Grover took over in 1957 was a free-and-clear, profitable enterprise, and his exertions were, in large measure, the reason for it. Without his shoulder at the wheel, I doubt that my father would have been able to drag the weight of that farm through the Flood, the Depression, and the drought. The year after the 1927 Flood Grover

Grover standing in tall cotton, 1946. *Author's collection.*

enrolled in Arkansas Agricultural and Mechanical College in
Monticello, but after a semester's attendance decided to come home
and help, although my father had somehow found enough money to
keep him there for at least another semester. Grover relished responsibility and had been trustworthy enough from childhood to be sent
out to supervise work crews of grown men by the age of twelve!
Furthermore, he loved farming and everything about it. Boss liked to
look at a cotton field ready to harvest and he loved pretty horses and
fine mules, but he despised cattle and would not give an orchard a
second glance. As I have mentioned before, he did not really *like* farming. Grover did not like horses and mules, but he liked everything
else, including cattle, fruit trees, all crops, cotton, corn, soybeans, and
rice as well as oats and lespedeza to feed the livestock. He liked to
read about farming, studied extensively about ways to improve production, and tried to implement them in the face of his partner's conservative approach. He believed in progress and in agricultural
diversity as a means to achieve it.

And above all, he believed in mechanization; he was innovative
in adapting machines to make work easier and invented machines
when the right equipment was not available. One such invention he

Grover, Fayree
and Casey, circa
1980. *Courtesy of
Albert Campbell.*

built and patented after the war was a gate equipped with an electric
eye that would automatically spray cows with pesticide when they
walked through it. It worked perfectly; the only problem lay in our
imperfect cows, half-wild range animals so terrified of this apparatus
they would have perished of thirst before going through it to the
water tank. (If he had thought about washing cars with it instead of
spraying cows, his fortune would have been made.) I can imagine the
enthusiasm in 1935 with which Grover must have embraced the new
challenge of whipping the the Bodine Place into shape.

Energetic and interested in everything, he always regretted that
he had not had the opportunity to finish college, a lack for which he
compensated with voracious reading and, thanks to Adolf Hitler,
extensive European travel. I remember that during the Depression, in

his spare time, he went all over the surrounding country selling Crosley radios for a merchant in Dumas named "Rock" Meador. Meador would pass his copies of *National Geographic* along to Grover, who read them cover to cover and shared them with the rest of us. During his service in England and Germany during World War II, he spent every available minute of leave visiting historic sites. Moreover, as an airplane mechanic, he was sent out with a crew to salvage parts from downed planes all over France, Germany, and Belgium as the allies progressed. On one such foray he was caught behind enemy lines in the Battle of the Bulge. Bob recalls Grover's telling him once that had it not been for the farm, he would have stayed in the air force after the war because he enjoyed travel so much. As an example of his mechanical ingenuity, a wrench he designed and made for use on airplane engines that prevented skinned knuckles was adopted by the air force. Every Sunday for years during the 1930s, there was a baseball game in our pasture, and the local teams used bats that Grover had made on a lathe in the farm shop.

In 1956, he married Fayree Sumrall of Dumas and, to the utter astonishment of everyone, decided to live in Dumas rather than build a house on the farm. His reasoning was that with the newly blacktopped road the trip out took only a few minutes. Furthermore, he was sure that since he was older, he would not outlive his wife and could not bear the thought of leaving her alone out there on the farm. Their only child, a son named Grover Cason Jones, called "Casey" for short, was born in 1960.

Grover's decision to live in town certainly did not indicate a fading interest in farming. It was clear from the beginning of his tenure as sole manager in 1957 that he had plans to tighten up whatever loose reins there were and make the farm an even more profitable enterprise than it had already become. He wanted to mechanize, moving from tenant farmers to salaried employees, and to expand his operation by leasing more land. According to his records, it apparently took him eight years to accomplish this. In 1961, he promoted Clyo Moore, who had been with us almost thirty years by that time, to the position of foreman. In 1962, he still had three tenants, two salaried tractor drivers, and the foreman who also operated a tractor as needed.

By 1966 he had no tenants at all, just the foreman, who also drove a tractor, and two tractor drivers. The tractor drivers were the sons of one of the former tenant farmers and were placed on year-round salary

Grover's carefully kept records for those years show the effects of his efforts on crop yields. With one exception, each year between 1961 and 1965 showed a higher yield for cotton. In 1961, 105 acres yielded 854 pounds per acre; in 1962, 110 acres yielded 553 pounds per acre; in 1963, 77.2 acres yielded 666 pounds per acre; in 1964, 106 acres yielded 936 pounds per acre; and in 1965, 80.6 acres yielded 959 pounds per acre. In 1964, the only one of these years in which he figured his profit from cotton in the ledger, his net proceeds on it totaled $30,487 or 30.9¢ per pound. Finally, there really did seem to be something at the end of the rainbow.[1] By 1964, soybeans had become a major crop as well as cotton, and that year the 200 acres planted in it yielded 3,330 bushels, or 16.6 bushels per acre. In 1965 he planted 230 acres that yielded 5,641 bushels, or 24.5 bushels per acre.

But it should also be noted that during these years he had two salaried jobs as well. He was Desha County Tax Assessor and also president and gin manager for the Pendleton Gin Association, a cooperative he had helped form after World War II, a position for which he received compensation during the autumn months when the gin was running.

For several years he leased the part of the Bodine Place that had been prepared for raising rice to some rice farmers from across the Arkansas River. Meanwhile, he began to level the rest of the farm so it could be irrigated efficiently and to lease land from neighbors to farm for himself. One of these was a 160-acre tract belonging to J. N. Holcombe, the man who had invited our family to stay with him until the 1927 Flood waters receded. Mr. Holcombe had lost his plantation, the Haywire Farm, in 1929 and bought 160 acres that he worked himself with a few farmhands. His success at this venture drew Grover's admiration and gave him a model for his own operations that was probably as influential as the lessons learned from his own predecessors, for Holcombe was a very careful manager who spent as little as possible and kept track of every cent that came in and went out. His philosophy, adopted by my brother, was to cut risk by cutting expense: "Better to make a bale to the acre at minimal cost than borrow the money to try to raise the production to a bale and a half with the risk of losing it all."

Since it was during Grover's lifetime that the giant steps in mechanization were taken that transformed cotton farming, this is as good a time as any to look at some figures that show just how dramatic those steps were. In 1840, it took 438 man-hours to produce a bale of cotton; in 1940, it took 182; in 1960, 47; and in 1970, 26. In 1840, it took 135 man-hours per acre of cotton; in 1940, 99; in 1960, 47; and in 1970, 24.[2] These figures are mere harbingers of things to come during Grover's son Casey's tenure.

Mechanizing allowed Grover to break the old cycle of tenant farming and crop liens that had plagued Southern agriculture from the beginning, for by the mid-1960s he had the resources to finance his own operations. But even for such a careful man, whose reach seldom exceeded his grasp, the comfort in which he found himself from this time until his death in 1991 did not assure him a state of anxiety-free ease. According to Casey, he still worried every year that the crop would fail and throw his family into destitution. The possible implications of every purchase, from major farm equipment to a child's bicycle, were carefully weighed on a balance against this awesome possibility, and the anxiety carefully passed along to his wife and son. Grover knew about the papers in those trunks: his grandfather Jones's bankruptcy declaration in 1869, the loss of his Grandmother Brown's land the same year, the countless land forfeitures for delinquent taxes, the devastation of a raging river, and the heartbreak of drought and the Great Depression, not to mention the fluctuation in cotton prices and the ballooning expense of trying to control the inexorable march of insects. He also knew about the good luck that had saved the place during his father's stewardship. In other words, he knew how fragile is the security of a farm, how foolish it is to think for an instant that it will last forever. It is worth noting, however, that he did not have a bad crop between the time he took over the farm in 1957 and 1985, the year he suffered a debilitating stroke and turned the operation over to Casey. Part of his success at farming was undoubtedly connected to the number of variables he was able to control that his predecessors had not been. The efficient use of fertilizers and pesticides along with judicious irrigation relieved many of the threats of nature that had dogged the farmers before him. However, his own hard work and constant supervision were equally as influential.

Near the beginning of this story I mentioned a sustaining dream that farmers must have to keep going: one year there will be a crop so good that the memory of it can warm the drafty floors of adversity for the rest of one's life. In 1948 such a year came for Boss; 1976 was the year of Grover's dream crop. It was the best year in the twenty-eight years of his tenure as manager, and probably the best in his lifetime. He planted 384 acres of cotton that yielded 234,783 pounds, for an average of 610 pounds per acre. The price that year was exceptionally good and since he had not signed a contract to sell at a predetermined figure, as he usually did, he was able to take advantage of the market price when he was ready to sell and received as much as 70¢ a pound for some of it. The farm's gross income that year was $188,930. The expenses amounted to $92,496, so Grover's net income from the farm in 1976 was $96,440.

His expenses are interesting because they show how he got the work done. There were, of course, no sharecroppers or renters by then. His labor force was salaried and included a foreman and two tractor drivers. Clyo Moore, the foreman, still lived on the place, but I believe the others did not, by that time. He also hired some machine work done by outside workers, and the cost of repairs on his own machinery was considerable. It is noteworthy that the cost of poison and fertilizer exceeded the cost of labor. Here is his list of expenses:

Labor	$17,846.34
Machine work hired	10,422.97
Seed	3,902.50
Supplies	485.56
Repairs	16,285.91
Fertilizer & poison	20,266.17
Fuel & oil	4,618.03
Taxes	6,595.51
Insurance	4,576.40

Utilities	413.73
Interest	4724.37
Business expenses	1,083.96
Miscellaneous expenses	46.00
Other farm expenses	1,222.61
Total Expenses	$92,490.06
Gross Income	$188,930.00
Net Profit	$96,440.00[3]

Needless to say, Grover did not rush out and buy a Cadillac and dig a swimming pool, as did some of his colleagues, and several years later when the plight of farmers became so dire that a protest, complete with a procession of tractors, was formed to march on Washington, he was heard to observe that if they all lived and operated their farms as frugally as *he* did, they wouldn't need to wear their tractors out in a protest. He probably did not believe that farmers should expect to drive Cadillacs and own swimming pools.

It was terrible but predictable that he had the stroke that eventually killed him while supervising the extrication of an overturned tractor from a ditch under the blazing sun in hundred-degree weather. He was seventy-four and well able to afford not to be in that field, but his style of management dictated that he be out there as long as he could crawl.

There are fewer written records for Grover and Casey's generations than for earlier times for several reasons. In the first place, record keeping was greatly simplified when there were no longer tenants. Under the old system, when "furnish" money was borrowed every first of March, exact records of its disbursement had to be kept. Uriah, Joseph, Boss, and then Grover until 1966 wrote down every penny lent to the tenants because they had to get it back before they, in turn, could repay their loans. It is interesting that they used a single-entry method of keeping books, meaning that only disbursements, not income, were usually noted. In the second place, there were fewer "important" papers to keep when the wolf was no longer at the door and legal threats no longer arrived with terrifying frequency in the mail. Since the manager no longer had to scrape the bottom of the barrel every year to pay taxes, the tax bills from the county were not so important. And, finally, modern custom simply does not encourage keeping every scrap of paper. With the road to the county seat paved, one can get there in a matter of minutes to look up a record and set matters straight. Members of my generation file birth certificates somewhere in their houses instead of making entries in the Bible. And I am certain the generation of our children does the same.

One thing Grover did do in 1976 was purchase the land that had slipped through Aunt Maggie's fingers in 1929, restoring some of Uriah's original two hundred acres to the farm, minus two lots retained by the sellers. We were all gratified to see it come back into the family.

As far as anyone knows, Grover was only moved to write one poem in his life. It was published in the local paper shortly after composition, and the preacher read it at his funeral. I think it pretty well sums up what he thought about agriculture:

Farming

Some men paint beautiful pictures upon canvas
　　　for which the whole world is grateful.
Other men build bridges and tall buildings
　　　for both beauty and utility.
And yet other men who plant and cultivate
　　　with the help of God
　　paint the most beautiful pictures of all
　　　upon the face of this good earth.
And when harvest time comes
　　　they erase all the beauty they have made.
But yet again, when planting time comes,
　　　Within their hearts they vow
　　　to grow a more beautiful picture
　　　than the one they grew before.

Grover was buried on June 7, 1991, in the family cemetery among the graves of his grandparents, parents, and some of his siblings as well as aunts, uncles, and cousins. It is hot in the Delta by June, but on that bright blue day there was a fine enough breeze to make the flag snap and to stir waves on Casey's catfish pond just below the cemetery. Everyone thought it was a beautiful day for Grover to be coming back to the farm.

Casey in front of his farm office, 2005. *Author's collection.*

Casey's house, 2006. *Author's collection.*

CHAPTER 6

The Casey Generation

1985–

A lthough Grover survived a massive stroke in 1985 with a clear mind, he was left partially paralyzed and was able to speak only with difficulty. It was clearly time for Casey to step in and take over as sole manager of the farm. He had been more or less in charge for several years, starting with the soybean part of the operation after graduation from high school in 1980 and moving into the cotton operation along the way. But the burden did not fall completely on his shoulders until 1985, when he was twenty-five years old, still single, and living at home. He had always been clear about his intentions to live on the farm, and when he married Larel Tanner in 1991, they built a house on the part of it still known as the "Bodine Place." Their daughter Kayla was born in 1993. As I write this in 2006, they still live there along with with Larel's son from a previous marriage, Neil Tanner.

Casey recalls that his father had given him an opportunity to do whatever he wanted to with his life and so was reluctant to invest much money in equipment and land leveling until he was sure that Casey truly intended to be a farmer, a matter about which there had never been any question in Casey's mind. He never imagined doing anything else. When his diligence with the soybeans eased his father's

Middle buster. *Courtesy of the Arkansas Post Museum, Gillett, Arkansas.*

The shovel points were set at a low angle to avoid deep cultivation that could damage the crop.

Gee-Whiz
(spring tooth cu

The jerky, kicking of the spring teeth weeds a free o

Double shovel. *Courtesy of the Plantation Agriculture Museum, Scott, Arkansas.*

Cultivator. *Courtesy of the Museum of the Arkansas Grand Prairie, Stuttgart, Arkansas.*

mind about his dedication to farming, Grover was ready to update the equipment and proceed with getting the land ready for successful irrigation, a step that he was not entirely sure would ever be worth what it would cost to do it. There were apparently the usual discussions between father and son with the conservative, older vision giving way reluctantly to the new. For example, Grover did not see the need for two-way radios connecting the trucks, tractors, and house until the system had been put in operation, nor did he own a tractor with a cab on it when Casey started farming. In terms of costs, the changes Casey wanted were a bit more drastic than Grover's spending five dollars for the first tractor he bought at an auction in 1933 over Boss's objections, but the principle was the same: modern farming required modern equipment, a point that the older farmer did not understand. Bigger tractors with comfortable cabs were necessary to keep drivers happy, as were better methods of communication when the farmer lived miles from his fields where machinery could be expected to break down. And it was clear to Casey that irrigation, expensive though it is to set up, is absolutely essential to

Casey's implement shed, 2004. *Author's collection.*

successful farming in the Delta. The ever increasing cost of production meant that they could no longer afford to depend on the whims
of nature. They could not wait for rain and expect to make a profit.

The operation Casey took over was a far cry from Uriah's venture in 1849; the wilderness had been tamed into a garden consisting
of 460 acres that Grover owned free and clear and 80 acres leased from
Pauline. Except for a few acres around the houses and in the edge of
the swamp, almost every foot of this land was in cultivation. In addition, Grover had been leasing land from neighbors and had maintained a good working relation with them, so Casey could continue
working their land as well as that belonging to his father and aunt.
By this time the flood control system in operation on the Mississippi
and Arkansas rivers could be reasonably expected to protect the area
from flooding, and the controls on variables that Grover had adopted
were further advanced by technology that produced ever bigger and
better equipment. Casey's intention from the beginning was to continue the process of mechanization with bigger equipment so that he
could work more land with fewer people.

In 1980 they had no tractors with cabs and no equipment wider
than six-row implements. Furthermore, most of the land was not

irrigated. In 1983 they bought a used John Deere tractor, a dirt buggy, and a laser with which to level all the ground for irrigation. They continued to upgrade their equipment, and by the year 2000, all the tractors had cabs, and the implements worked eight rows at a time. (Eleven quarter-mile rows make an acre, so they could plow an acre in a little over five minutes.) Casey owned five tractors: one with 190 horsepower, one with 160 horsepower, two more with about 100 horsepower, and then a much smaller one for general utility. He also had a cotton picker, a combine for harvesting grain, and an eighteen-wheel truck as well as a pick-up truck for his constant use. The replacement value of this equipment in 2000, if bought new, would have been at least a million dollars, but Casey was astute at buying good equipment at auction sales and figured his equipment had probably cost him half that. The labor force required to run it consisted of two full-time drivers on year-round salary and one temporary one during cotton planting time. In addition, two Mexicans came in June and stayed through the harvest to do manual tasks such as chopping cotton where needed and then stomping the cotton down in the trailers after it was picked. Casey did not usually drive a tractor himself, its having been more important for him to keep an eye on the entire operation so he could step in quickly when there were breakdowns. With this equipment and labor force, in 2000, he farmed 1,250 acres, with 550 planted in cotton, 400 in soybeans, and 300 in wheat.

When Casey began farming, realizing that he leaned heavily on his father for advice and that he would have nobody to consult in the event of his father's death, he decided to keep careful records of his day-to-day operations so that he would have something of his own to consult. Beginning in 1980, he kept a notebook in which he recorded every night what had been done in each individual field that day. Casey's notebooks are interesting for the similarities and differences they show between his methods, using relatively advanced equipment, and his grandfather Boss's methods. It is easy to imagine that it resembles the speeding up of film. In Chapter 3, I quoted Jodie's description of the process of cultivating cotton with the equipment used in the 1930s, which had not changed much since 1860. Here are

Casey's notes regarding the work required in 1981 on one of the home fields in the original plot that would have been worked by Uriah, Joseph, Boss, and Grover as well. It should be noted that the work in 1981 was done with relatively old-fashioned equipment, as Casey had not yet modernized his father's operation. The tractors were cab-less, and the equipment worked only six rows at a time. Still, the difference is staggering.

Lloyd Field #1 (by highway)

12/24/80	Cut cotton stalks, subsoiled N.E. to S.W.
1/12/81	Disked
3/26/81	Vibershanked
4/6/81	Used Do-all. Bedded up
4/10/81	Fertilized with nitrogen, rehipped at same time with Do-all.
4/25/81	Planted cotton DOL PL 61, put out Treflan and Cottoran at same time
5/7/81	Plowed with Dickyvator, no spray
5/25/81	Plowed cotton with Dickyvator, no spray
6/12/81	Plowed cotton with Dickyvator, no spray
6/22/81	Plowed cotton with Dickyvator, put out spray where needed, Cottoran and MSMA
6/26/81	Ran Wickbar over Johnson grass
7/8/81	Plowed cotton with Dickyvator without fenders, no spray
9/2/81	Put out defoliant, Def 4 Paraquat
10/1/81	Started picking on this field today. It was second field we picked
10/2/81	Finished picking on this field. Picked 15 bales

So the entire operation for Lloyd Field #1 took 20 whole or partial days that year. The yield was 1.85 bales per acre, so if the tractor driver worked the usual 11 hours a day, the man-hours required to produce a bale of cotton had been reduced to about 5! This can be compared to 438 in 1860, and 27 in 1970!

As equipment got bigger and more efficient over the next twenty years, this time was shortened considerably, but the farmer making the 1981 crop was still essentially cultivating the land as his predecessors had done since the invention of the plow. Chemicals were used to control insects and some weeds, but the method of cultivation was the same, only faster, as tractors and implements had improved. The modern "Dickyvator" had replaced the cultivator that had replaced the double shovel that had replaced the single-pointed plow that had replaced the hoe that had replaced the sharp stick, but the age-old principle remained: the soil had to be broken and bedded up before planting and then after the crop was up, tilled periodically until "layby" and then infrequently after that until harvest. Moreover, in 1981, some hand labor was still needed for cleanup chopping in the fields and for tromping cotton down in the trailers after the mechanical picker dumped it in. The next phase in the history of cotton farming was entirely different and depended on a level of technology and efficiency undreamed of only a few years before.

By using genetically engineered, Roundup Ready seeds, Casey made his 2004 crop without putting a plow point in the ground, except for the hippers and soil-openers on the planter. This is his description of the process of raising cotton and soybeans in 2004:

> I guess I started using Roundup-ready bean seeds about 1990 but 2004 was the first year I farmed Roundup-ready cotton. Cotton and soybeans have just been bred to yield more every year and now you have to expect two bales to the acre to stay in business. You can just spray Roundup over the top and never have to plow. You kill everything but the cotton and soybeans. Since they came out with that, things have gotten gradually better.
>
> If the ground is hipped in the fall and fertilized, in the spring you go in there and spray Roundup before you plant, roll the bed flat and plant on top of the plant bed. The planter has two disc blades that throw the dirt back, set to make a trench as deep as you want to plant, then a container for the seeds set to plant them exactly as you want to. You can plant two, three, four seeds in a hill, as many as you want. I put four seeds in, twelve inches apart. Now that cotton seed is around $300 a sack, some people put three seeds in and some, maybe

two, but I never skimp on seeds. Then, after the seeds drop, two more disc wheels cover them up and a roller tamps the top of the bed down. We planted eight rows at a time, at five miles an hour, so it took maybe seven or eight minutes to plant an acre. [An acre is eleven quarter-mile rows.] After that it's just maintenance: spraying pesticides and insecticides as well as fertilizer, and irrigating when necessary. When the cotton plants get five leaves on them, you can't spray from the top, so you have to spray under the plants, and there's a fitting on the equipment for that. Roundup kills everything but morning glory and stuns that so it stops growing. This method of farming is absolutely consistent.

When cotton-picking time comes, we use module builders to keep it in and take it to the gin. Each one has a hydraulic tromper, so you don't need a man to get in there and tromp the cotton down. The cotton picker dumps the cotton directly into it, or you can use a boll-buggy to take the cotton from the picker to the module builder. You can pull it around from field to field, if you need to. This is a big trailer that will hold fifteen bales and you can throw a $65 tarp over it and let it sit there for a month. The advantage is that it can wait at the gin until they have time to gin it, and the truck driver doesn't have to wait too. And, you can go to the gin less often.

The best pounds to the acre Daddy made was 650 bales on 400 acres; that's a little over a bale to the acre, for five-hundred pound bales; two men picked that crop. By 2000, you had to *expect* two bales to the acre. In 2004, the last year I farmed, a lot of the fields made three bales to the acre. Some, more than that, but it started raining and was real wet, so by the time we got through, we were picking only a bale and a half to the acre.

Casey's daily logbook for 2004, included in the appendix below, reads like science fiction. The age-old method of tilling the soil has been replaced by a process of adjusting machinery to plant the seeds and then measuring and distributing poison that kills noxious weeds and insects. If sufficient moisture does not fall from the sky, it is supplied by irrigation.

If we count the number of passes made by a tractor and equipment traveling at five miles an hour over an acre of cotton in Lloyd

Field #1 (referred to in this notebook as "Lloyd Highway"), the field used above to calculate the number of man-hours needed to produce a bale of cotton in 1981 and add a few miscellaneous minutes for loading and hauling to the gin plus the few seconds it took for the two airplane passes also used to put out poison, we find that by 2004, some sixty-four to seventy-five minutes were required to work an acre of cotton. Assuming an average yield of two bales per acre, it took less than one man-hour in the field to produce a bale of cotton (and, of course, a million dollars worth of equipment that did not malfunction too badly, a manager who knew how to do everything, skilled tractor drivers who could handle the equipment, and the cooperation of the weather.)

The 2004 crop marked the end of Casey's row-crop farming. He had brought the farm into the modern age with remarkable success and then a few years bad enough to scare him came along. This is the way he describes it:

My best year was 1997. I bought myself a new truck and Larel a new Tahoe. Bought a late-model big tractor. Then the bad years started. I lost money for the first time in '98 and then for a couple of years after that. '98, '99, 2000 were scary. When you have two or three bad years in a row it'll just about take the sap out of you. You can see the end coming.

I decided to quit for a number of reasons. Technology was one of them. These new tractors have computers on them now and in a year or two I don't know where you are going to find somebody who can operate one. I didn't have this on my tractors but the newer ones have a guidance system so that after you turn the tractor round at the end of the row, it drives itself and the driver can turn his swivel seat around and face the back and watch his equipment until it's time to turn the thing around again! So it takes someone who knows what they are doing to handle one. Labor is a problem. Most drivers now are Mexicans who go back to Mexico at the end of the season. There are still some local people, both black and white, who want to work on a farm, but not many.

Another reason for quitting when I did was that I knew that there were still farmers around here who would rent my land and in a few years I doubt that will be true. Farmers are going out of business right and left. This is February, and every day this month, except Sundays, the auction company that handled my auction has a sale somewhere in Arkansas.

Another reason was that I don't know how long the government subsidies will last, and we can't do without them. And as important as anything else in my reasoning was the price of cotton. Cotton was selling yesterday for 55 cents a pound. That's about what it was in the eighties when I started farming.[1]

Another factor entered Casey's calculations that 2004 was a good time to give up cotton and soybean farming. He had an extraordinary piece of bad luck that fall that might have ruined him: his cotton picker broke down in October and was out of the field for some three weeks. Then the rains came, as he mentions above. He was able to get the machine repaired, the fields dried enough for picking to resume, and he salvaged his crop. But, as his notebook shows, it took two months to finish the picking. And he really needed a new cotton picker, which would cost around $350,000, money that would have to be borrowed. With this staring him in the face as well as the factors he lists above, he decided to quit. It was a terrible decision for him to make. In the spring of 2005, he had an auction and sold his equipment. His uncles and aunts, who have acted as a Greek chorus for his entire life, thought he had done the right thing.

In its dependence on help from the government in the form of subsidies, Casey's operation was similar to Boss's. As he said, he would not have been able to stay in business without them. Here is a summary of the subsidies he received from 1995–2003:

Crop	Crop Payments
Cotton Subsidies	$477,994
Rice Subsidies	119,858
Wheat Subsidies	28,911
Soybean Subsidies	22,994
Sorghum Subsidies	10,993
Total	$660,750[2]

But giving up the row crops did not mean that Casey would quit farming altogether. Like Grover in his search for diversity, in 2000, he decided to expand his aquaculture operation and had two nine-acre catfish ponds dug near his house. (He had put in a pond near the cemetery years before that seemed to lose a lot of fish to local fishermen.) The irony of the situation was not lost on any of us: the best way to make a profit now on the richest land in the world meant digging a hole and planting catfish in it. But it is profitable and requires very little labor. Here is Casey's explanation of the process of catfish farming:

> The two ponds are nine acres each. As soon as they were built, I put about 6500 head of 6 inch fingerlings in there and they cost a cent and a half an inch. And I started feeding them and at the same time the next year I put about 4,000 head in, and then the next year the first fish I put in there were ready to sell. So each year I've got a crop of fish ready to sell and then I go back and put in fingerlings each year so I always have a crop of fish to sell in the spring.
>
> I have a fish feeder with a gravity flow that puts the feed into a blower that blows the pellets out about sixty feet over the water. Takes about an hour a day. In the summer when the weather gets warm, they have to have oxygen in the night. So somebody has to be here to turn the electric paddle wheels on and then turn them off about nine o'clock in the morning. If one of those paddle wheels quits they may all come up and die, and that has happened. There's not much worse than that. It takes about three days for them to disintegrate or get eaten by turtles and for the smell to dissipate.
>
> The only time it takes labor is when I seine them and it takes four or five people to seine each pond. And that's about all there is to it. With eighteen acres of catfish and the rent from the land, I may do even better than I did farming the whole place myself.[3]

I asked Casey if he would encourage anybody to go into farming now, and he said he would not. His daughter, Kayla, is leaning toward being a lawyer at the moment. Casey thinks that is just fine.

Reunion of Boss and Zena's descendants, 1997. *Courtesy of Dana Jones.*

CHAPTER 7

Conclusion

S o this is the way it stands in 2006, 157 years into the Jones
family's ownership of the farm: some of us still own it, but
nobody lives in the house. Casey and Pauline own the land, but
Pauline has moved to an assisted-living facility, and her daughter, Sue
Lloyd Ray, who lives in Pine Bluff, will inherit the house. It is empty
now, and it is unlikely that she or her children will ever live in it.
Pauline's son Billy and his son have homes within a stone's throw of
the old house, but they are not farmers. Casey and his family live on
the Bodine Place, where he runs his catfish operation. And both
Pauline and Casey lease their fields to a neighbor who continues to
raise cotton and soybeans on it.

And we are left with the question of what it meant to us to have
that farm in the family over the years, considering the effort it has
taken to keep it. And the answer, of course, is that it meant a great
deal, for as surely as we shaped the farm, it shaped us. It is not enough
to simply say that we loved it; it gave us the landscape of our minds.
In this part of the world, where ownership of land is paramount,
this farm has been a source of pride and stability from the very
beginning. It is easy to imagine what it meant to Uriah and Joseph
in 1860 as they envisioned themselves rising in the social scale to
the planter class. For those who came later, there was the added

aspect of romance, as the achievements of the first generations became legendary and mythical. It nourished our fantasies, for in the tales of those vanished generations lay a certain realm of magic that gave us, throughout the hard years, a well of romance to draw upon that gave us pride and confidence. It did not matter a whit that the magic and romance lay in the tales, not in the sweat and pain of reality. But it meant something that they had chopped that farm out of the wilderness, held on to it, and made it feed and clothe us through thick and thin. They had survived the onslaughts of nature and war and lived to tell about it. And the stories wove a cocoon of protection around us that nurtured our souls. The trials of the present were made to seem manageable when compared to the trials of the past. People dead long before we were born were spoken of as if they had just stepped out of the room. Things that had happened to them, their hopes and aspirations, became part of our dream too. Joseph's stories of the Civil War, passed down to us by our father and Aunt Sallie, seemed as real as if we had been there ourselves. The disasters and triumphs and the bumper crop years as well as the floods and droughts were all woven into the stuff of our imaginations because they were tied to people who were tied to a certain place, our place.

And the solid foundation under all this was the land itself, which, for us, became the benchmark for what well tended, flat fields should look like. I remember raising the shade on a train going across northern Germany one night in 1962 and remarking that the field we were passing out there in the moonlight looked like the field one sees from the front porch, "Lloyd #1," as Casey named it in his records. Again, on another trip in Russia, between the airport and Moscow, I saw another field just like it.

Uriah and Sarah's descendants have followed diverse paths. Members of the family in the last two generations alone include teachers, university professors, government officials, an electrician, postal workers, physicians, nurses, a lawyer, a psychologist, businessmen, an accountant, housewives, a dietitian, missionaries, and two farmers. We meet annually to share a meal and to congratulate ourselves for still being alive, and as we cross the state for this reunion in our Cadillacs, Mercedes, Buicks, and SUVs of one kind or another, we might well wonder what Uriah and Sarah would think about us. Have things turned out for this family as they hoped they would when they came to the Delta? Are we and what we have become what they were searching for?

I think so, but that being the case, a reader could wonder why I chose the Thomas Hardy poem, "During Wind and Rain," as epigraph and title for this narrative. Why set an elegiac tone for a story of success? As I have already mentioned, the poem first came to mind in reference to a photograph of Joseph and the family taken at a happy time, before a series of disasters fell upon them that broke the old man, almost lost him the farm, and ruptured the family circle as well. But seeing that part of the tale unfold would not justify an elegiac tone for the whole text; the family adjusted to tragedy and loss, the farm was saved, they survived.

And it is certainly sad that nobody in the family is following the yearly course of planting cotton and seeing it through the harvest. As long as a family member was running the farm, all of us in my generation, wherever we were, followed that progression in our minds and remarked on it to our children. Now our connection with the land in that particular way is gone. After Casey's generation, nobody will even remember it. (Do catfish really count?)

And of course it is heart-breaking to see the house, empty now of the only family that ever lived in it, beginning to look run-down and derelict, as vacant houses do.

And yet, while these particular instances are enough to justify sadness on the level of the family's reminiscences, even taken altogether they surely do not hold up the weight of elegy Hardy's poem lays on the entire narrative. For that, we need to look at the Jones family's story in the context of the bigger picture of the agrarian dreams that made America, for it is there that one finds the root of this sense of sadness and loss: at the very beginning of the venture in the difference I mentioned near the start of this account between the ideals for this particular farm and those of "family" farms in other parts of the country. The model for the ideal here was the plantation, including slavery, for the cheap labor necessary to make money by raising cotton. (Although Thomas Jefferson may have visualized a nation of happy and successful yeoman farmers, he was not one himself, and the yeomen, probably to a man, would have preferred to be in his shoes.) This family, and thousands like it, wanted to move the South westward, and the results of striving to achieve those ideals are engraved on both the environment and the very soul of this nation. Both nature and our social structure have been heavily marked by the crack in the golden bowl that held our particular dream.

For, granted that all agriculture, by definition, is a perversion of nature, the limits seem to have been stretched here. With the heightened consciousness of twenty-first-century environmentalism, it is not possible to look at those fields stretching to the horizons and not consider the ravishing of nature required to achieve them. This was, indeed, a Garden of Eden, and the serpent, built into it from the beginning, was slavery, which brings us, finally, to the real reason for the elegiac tone in the narrative of the Jones family and its farm: the crack in the bowl was the flaw in the dream itself, the acceptance of slavery as the means to achieve it. Was it not, after all, our version of the American agrarian dream that produced the nightmare of race relations that the entire nation is still struggling to wake from? Without the promise of those vast cotton lands in the Delta and the rest of the Southern frontier in the 1830s and 1840s that could not be fulfilled without cheap labor, slavery might well have withered on the vine of the depleted soil of the eastern seaboard. In that case, our dream would have been different—and so would our farm and our story and perhaps, also, the story of the nation.

Casey's Field Notebook for 2004

ALL FIELDS

4/4/04   Put out 1 oz. Aim & 1 qt Roundup on all cotton & bean ground with hoods & 1 tyo cycle.

4/19/04   Rehipped all bean ground on old beds & rolled beds.

PLANTING COTTON

4/20/04   Started planting cotton on Lloyd & 2 40's on Sharp. Planted DEPL 555 treated with Cruiser & Plotojay. Put out 1 pint of Prowl behind planter with 1 pint of Ammo for cutworms, speed is 5mph, 8th gear, pressure is 82 PSI. 30 acre load mixed 4 gal. Prowl & 1 pint Ammo. Sprockets were set on 24 front & 16 back, 10 lbs seed to acre. Will need rain to come up.

4/26/04   Planted Lake Bank field with Stoneville 5599 RR BR. Cemetery, Gibbs & Lloyd on Highway, Hill, Big field on Sharp and Holcomb place, all same 5599.

5/6/04   Planted DEPL 436 RRnon B+ BG on Shop field.

COTTON SPRAYING FOR WEEDS

5/6/04   Sprayed Lake 30, Cemetery & Lloyd on back with only 1 qt roundup.

5/6/04   Sprayed both 40's on Sharp place with 1 qt roundup.

5/11/04   Sprayed Gibbs & Lloyd on Highway, Hill, Holcomb, Shop & Sharp big field with 1 qt roundup.

5/21/04   Sprayed Lake, Cemetery, Lloyd on back with 1 qt roundup.

5/24/04   Sprayed Sharp 40's & big field with roundup & Briden.

5/24/04	Sprayed Hill, Holcomb & Shop fields with roundup & Staple Soybean Planting.
5/7/04	Started planting beans today. Planted Armor 56J6 by Office, Long rows on highway, Holcomb place, Hill place & by Fred's.
5/8/04	Planted split Field, By Tree, Mosby field.
5/11/04	Planted Lloyd on highway, Kennedy, Back 40 & Mud Hole. V8 on all but Mud Hole. It was J6. Sprockets were same as cotton, 24 front—16 back.
5/21/04	Sprayed cotton with Staple: mixed 2 6oz bags & 1 gal oil to 300 gals water. Sprayed in 9th gear, pressure at 25 on 4450 #2. 371/2 acres per load.
5/24/04	Sprayed soybeans with 1 1/3 pts roundup.
5/26/04	Sprayed beans.
6/7/04	Put out 90 units @ 2lbs of Boron with Coulter rig. [fertilizer]
6/8/04	Put Roundup and Aim in middles.
6/18/04	1 pt roundup & ? oz Aim [per acre]
6/04	In June put out 4 oz Pixor 555 on Lloyd and 4 oz 555 on Sharp fields.
7/4/04	Put out ? lb optnene & 8 oz Pixar on all cotton with airplane.
7/16/04	Put out Ammo, Orthane. Layby. 8200 tractor, front tank sprays under cotton: 5 gal Divron, ? bottle Aim, 3 jugs roundup, Pressure at 25. 60 acres per load. Back tank sprayed middles: 4 gal Divron, ? bottle Aim, 3 jugs roundup. Pressure at 30. 40 acres per load. Sprayed both 40's on Sharp place & lower ends of Big Field with 10 oz Select & ?% Surfacant with airplane.

IRRIGATION

7/13/04	Started watering cotton by Shop and on Hill Place
8/20/04	Got 1 inch rain and stopped watering cotton for year
7/4/04	Stopped watering beans for year

NOTES

Introduction

1. S.V. Daniel to his sister Alice, Harriet Bailey Bullock Daniel Collection, Williams R. Perkins Library, Duke University.

2. Harriet Bailey Bullock Daniel, *A Remembrance of Eden: Harriet Bailey Bullock Daniel's Memories of a Frontier Plantation in Arkansas, 1849–1872,* ed. Margaret Jones Bolsterli (Fayetteville: University of Arkansas Press, 1993).

3. Shirley Abbott, *Womenfolks: Growing Up Down South* (New Haven: Ticknor & Fields, 1983), 185.

CHAPTER I
The Place They Came To

1. *Arkansas: General Land Office Automated Records Project.* CD-ROM. Bureau of Land Management, Washington, DC, 1993.

2. *Arkansas: General Land Office Automated Records Project.*

3. Thomas Nuttall, *A Journal of Travels Into The Arkansas Territory* (Readex Microprint Corporation, 1966), 72-73.

4. "Letters of Cassandra Sawyer Lockwood," *Chronicles of Oklahoma* 33 (1955): 206-07.

5. George C. Camp to My Dear Sister, 1 April 1851, Camp Letters, Special Collections, University of Arkansas at Fayetteville Library.

6. James W. Leslie, *Land of Cypress and Pine* (Little Rock: Rose, 1976), 40.

7. *Pine Bluff Commercial,* 31 January 1913, 8. Quoted in Leslie, *Land of Cypress and Pine,* 40.

8. John Kerr to James Graham, 25 May 1851, Small Manuscripts Collection, Arkansas History Commission, Little Rock.

9. Mark Twain, *Life on the Mississippi* (New York: Harper & Brothers, 1917), 285-86.

10. Henry Morton Stanley, *Autobiography* (Boston: Houghton Mifflin, 1909), 156.

CHAPTER 2
The Uriah Generation 1849-1872

1. *Arkansas: General Land Office Automated Records Project.*

2. U.S. Bureau of the Census, *7th Census of the United States,* 1850, University of Arkansas at Fayetteville Library, roll 26.

3. U.S. Bureau of the Census, *7th Census of the United States,* 1850.

Manuscript Census, Special Collections, University of Arkansas at Fayetteville
Library.

4. Francis Terry Leak Diary, quoted in William Kauffman Scarborough, *The
Overseer: Plantation Management in the Old South* (Athens: University of Georgia
Press, 1966), 25.

5. Scarborough, *The Overseer,* 27.

6. Author's interview with Paul Stacy, June 1987.

7. Donald P. McNeilly, *The Old South Frontier: Cotton Plantations and the
Formation of Arkansas Society, 1819-1861* (Fayetteville: University of Arkansas Press,
2000), 59-60.

8. Desha County Tax Records, 1852-1862, Arkansas History Commission,
Little Rock, microfilm roll 68.

9. U.S. Bureau of the Census, *8th Census of the United States,* 1860,
University of Arkansas at Fayetteville Library, microfilm roll 18.

10. Desha County Tax Records.

11. "The Amnesty Oaths Taken by Residents of Desha County, Arkansas
Following The End Of The Civil War," *Programs of the Desha County Historical
Society,* 17 (Fall 1992): 20.

12. Donald Holley, "The Plantation Heritage: Agriculture in the Arkansas
Delta," in *The Arkansas Delta,* Jeannie Whayne and Willard B. Gatewood, eds.
(Fayetteville: University of Arkansas Press, 1993), 242–43.

13. Capt. E. G. Barker to B. W. Thomas, Field Office Records: Napoleon,
Bureau of Refugees, Freedmen, and Abandoned Lands, Washington, DC, record
group 105, microfilm roll 15.

14. Carl T. Moneyhon, *The Impact of the Civil War and Reconstruction on
Arkansas* (Fayetteville: University of Arkansas Press, 2002), 239.

15. Injunction, Desha County Chancery Court, October 1866, Desha
County Courthouse, Arkansas City, AR, 44.

16. Moneyhon, *The Impact,* 223.

17. Moneyhon, *The Impact,* 250.

18. Desha County Tax Records.

19. Reports of Capt. J. C. Predmore, Freedmen's Bureau, Little Rock, AR,
microfilm roll 15.

20. Warranty deed, Uriah Jones to Joseph Jones, Deed Book B, 1868, Desha
County Courthouse, Arkansas City, AR, 6.

21. Joseph H. Jones's pocket book, Jones family papers.

22. Deed Record Book D, Desha County Courthouse, 270.

23. U.S. Bureau of the Census, *9th Census of the United States,* 1870, Schedule
3, Desha County, Arkansas.

24. Donald P. McNeilly, *The Old South Frontier,* 62.

25. U. S. Bureau of the Census, *Historical Statistics of the United States: Colonial
Times to 1970,* 500, quoted in Donald Holley, *The Second Great Emancipation*
(Fayetteville: University of Arkansas Press, 2000), 14.

26. *Arkansas: General Land Office Automated Records Project.*

CHAPTER 3
The Joseph Generation

1. *Biographical and Historical Memoirs of Southern Arkansas,* (Chicago: Goodspeed, 1890), 1027.

2. Joseph H. Jones, "Sketch of My Army Life from 1861 to 1865," Jones family papers.

3. "The Amnesty Oaths," 20.

4. Deed Record Book B, 1868, Desha County Courthouse, 192–94.

5. Chancery Court Record Book A-1865, 1870, Desha County Courthouse, 287.

6. Deed Record Book G, 1858, Desha County Courthouse, 312. Deed Record Book C, 1858, Desha County Courthouse, 269.

7. Orville Taylor, *Negro Slavery in Arkansas* (Durham, NC: Duke University Press, 1958) 78–81.

8. Deed and Mortgage Record A-1865, Desha County Courthouse, 215–16.

9. Deed Record Book B, 1868, Desha County Courthouse, 192–94. Chancery Court Record Book A-1865, Desha County Courthouse, 34, 327.

10. Elizabeth Payne, "What Ain't I Been Doing?," in *The Arkansas Delta,* 130–31.

11. Maury County Clerk's certificate, Jones family papers.

12. Will T. Watkins to Joseph H. Jones, 9 June 1893, Jones family papers.

13. John Kitely to Joseph H. Jones, 12 April 1896, Jones family papers.

14. U.S. Bureau of the Census, *10th Census of the United States,* 1880, University of Arkansas at Fayetteville Library, roll 58.

15. U.S. Bureau of the Census, *10th Census of the United States,* Manuscript Census, 1880, University of Arkansas at Fayetteville Library.

16. Arkansas Department of Public Instruction, teacher's license, Jones family papers.

17. L. C. Furbish to Joseph H. Jones, 29 March 1904, Jones family papers.

18. Margaret A. Frierson, 3 June 1861, Wills 1851–1898, Tennessee State Library and Archives, microfilm roll 193.

19. Margaret Jones Bolsterli, *Born in the Delta,* 109–21. "Soul Food," *The Encyclopedia of Southern Culture* (Chapel Hill: University of North Carolina Press, 1989), 701.

20. Sallie Owen Shaifer to Sallie Jones, 31 October 1901, Jones family papers.

21. Sallie Owen Shaifer to Sallie Jones, 8 June 1893, Jones family papers.

22. U.S. Bureau of the Census, *12th Census of the United States,* 1900, University of Arkansas at Fayetteville Library, roll 84.

23. Robertson to Joseph H. Jones, 1 April 1904, Jones family papers.

24. Yowell & Williams to Joseph H. Jones, 11 February 1904, Jones family papers.

25. *Biographical and Historical Memoirs,* 1027.

CHAPTER 4

The Boss and Sallie Generation 1906–1957

1. Title abstract, 9 December 1910, Jones family papers.

2. Jack Bernhardt to Sallie V. Jones, Jones family papers.

3. Bank of Dumas mortgage note, March 1908, Jones family papers.

4. Sallie V. Jones Tax Records, Jones family papers.

5. U.S. Bureau of the Census, *13th Census of the United States*, 1910, University of Arkansas at Fayetteville Library, roll 7.

6. U.S. Bureau of the Census, *14th Census of the United States*, 1920, University of Arkansas at Fayetteville Library, roll 61.

7. Desha County Bank Chattel and Crop Mortgage, 5 March 1925, Jones family papers.

8. McNeely Motor Company Bills of Sale, 24 July 1918, Jones family papers.

9. Grover Jones, "Origin of Pea Ridge Name Lost," *Programs of the Desha County Historical Society* vol (season 1973): 36.

10. Joseph Gallatin Jones, memoir, Jones family papers

11. Commissioner's report, Chancery I, 1929, Desha County Courthouse, 161.

12. McKennon-Jones, contract for sale, 8 November 1929, Jones family papers.

13. Desha County Deed Book 62, 1933, Desha County Courthouse, 270.

14. Richard H. Bodine to G. C. Jones, 25 November 1935, Jones family papers.

15. Bodine-Jones lease agreement, Jones family papers.

16. Bodine-Jones correspondence, Jones family papers. G. C. Jones tax receipts, Jones family papers.

17. Bodine-Jones correspondence, 7 December 1938, Jones family papers.

18. Joseph Gallatin Jones, memoir.

19. Donald Holley, *The Second Great Emancipation*, 9.

20. Environmental Working Group Farm Subsidy Database, http://www.ewg.org/16080/farm/persondetail.php7custnumber=005193 (accessed 1 March 2006).

21. IRS form 1065, 1942, Jones family papers

22. Jeannie Whayne, "Interview with Billy Lee Riley," *Arkansas Historical Quarterly* LV, no. 3 (Autumn 1966): 310.

23. Jeannie Whayne, "Interview with Billy Lee Riley," 304.

24. Grover Cleveland Jones, farm ledger, 1951, Jones family papers.

Chapter 5
The Grover Generation 1957–1985

1. Grover Cason Jones, farm ledger, 1965, Jones family papers
2. Donald Holley, *The Second Great Emancipation*, 14.
3. Grover and Fayree Jones, IRS Form 1040 and Grover's worksheets, 1976, Jones family papers.

Chapter 6
The Casey Generation 1985–

1. Author's interview with Casey Jones, June 2006.
2. Environmental Working Group Farm Subsidy Database, http://www.ewg.org (accessed 1 March 2006).
3. Author's interview with Casey Jones.

BIBLIOGRAPHY

"Amnesty Oaths Taken by Residents of Desha County, Arkansas Following the End of the Civil War." *Programs of the Desha County Historical Society.* 17 (Fall 1992).

Abbott, Shirley. *Womenfolks: Growing Up Down South.* New Haven: Ticknor & Fields, 1983.

Arkansas: General Land Office Automated Records Project. CD-ROM. Washington, DC: Bureau of Land Management, 1993.

Barker, E. G. Letter to B. W. Thomas. Field Office Records: Napoleon. Washington, DC: Bureau of Refugees, Freedmen and Abandoned Lands, record group 105, mircofilm roll 15.

Biographical and Historical Memoirs of Southern Arkansas. Chicago: Goodspeed, 1890.

Bolsterli, Margaret Jones, ed. *A Remembrance of Eden: Harriet Bailey Bullock Daniel's Memories of a Frontier Plantation in Arkansas, 1849–1872.* Fayetteville: University of Arkansas Press, 1993.

Bolsterli, Margaret Jones. *Born in the Delta: Reflections on the Making of a Southern White Sensibility.* Knoxville: University of Tennessee Press, 1991.

Camp, George C. Letter to his sister. Camp Letters. Special Collections. University of Arkansas at Fayetteville Library. (Hereafter referred to as UAF).

Chancery Court Record Book A-1865. 1870. Desha County Courthouse. Arkansas City, AR.

Daniel, S.V. Letter to Alice. Harriet Bailey Bullock Daniel Collection. William R. Perkins Library, Duke University.

Deed Record Book B. 1868. Desha County Courthouse.

Deed Record Book D. 1868. Desha County Courthouse.

Deed Record Book G. 1858. Desha County Courthouse.

Desha County Tax Records, 1852–1862. Little Rock: Arkansas History Commission, microfilm roll 68.

Encyclopedia of Southern Culture. Chapel Hill: University of North Carolina Press, 1989.

Environmental Working Group Farm Subsidy Database. http://*www.ewg.org* (accessed 1 March 2006.)

Holley, Donald. "The Plantation Heritage: Agriculture in the Arkansas Delta." *The Arkansas Delta.* Jeannie Whayne and Willard B. Gatewood, eds. Fayetteville: University of Arkansas Press, 1993.

———. *The Second Great Emancipation*. Fayetteville: University of Arkansas Press, 2000.

Jones Family Papers. Special Collections. UAF.

Kerr, John. Letter to James Graham. Small Manuscripts Collection. Little Rock: Arkansas History Commission.

Leslie, James W. *Land of Cypress and Pine*. Little Rock: Rose, 1976.

Lockwood, Cassandra Sawyer. "Letters of Cassandra Sawyer Lockwood." *Chronicles of Oklahoma* 33 (1955).

McNeilly, Donald P. *The Old South Frontier: Cotton Plantations and the Formation of Arkansas Society 1819–1861*. Fayetteville: University of Arkansas Press, 2000.

Moneyhon, Carl T. *The Impact of the Civil War and Reconstruction on Arkansas*. Baton Rouge: Louisiana State University Press, 1994.

Nuttall, Thomas. *A Journal of Travels Into The Arkansas Territory*. Readex Microprint Corporation, 1966.

Scarborough, William Kauffman. *The Overseer: Plantation Management in the Old South*. Athens: University of Georgia Press, 1966.

Stanley, Henry Morton. *Autobiography*. Boston: Houghton Mifflin, 1909.

Wills 1851–1898. Nashville: Tennessee State Library and Archives, microfilm roll 193.

Twain, Mark. *Life on the Mississippi*. New York: Harper & Brothers, 1917.

U.S. Bureau of the Census. *7th Census of the United States*. 1850. UAF, microfilm roll 26.

———. *7th Census of the United States*. Manuscript Census. 1850. Special Collections. UAF.

———. *8th Census of the United States*. 1860. UAF, microfilm roll 18.

———. *9th Census of the United States*. 1870. UAF, microfilm roll 37.

———. *10th Census of the United States*. 1880. UAF, microfilm roll 58.

———. *12th Census of the United States*. 1900. UAF, microfilm roll 84.

———. *13th Census of the United States*. 1910. UAF, microfilm roll 7.

———. *14th Census of the United States*. 1920. UAF, microfilm roll 61.

Whayne, Jeannie. "Interview with Billy Lee Riley." *Arkansas Historical Quarterly*, 3, LV: 1966.

INDEX

During Wind and Rain is the second of three books by Margaret Jones Bolsterli about growing up in Desha County, Arkansas. The first, *Born in the Delta*, was published by the University of Arkansas Press in 2000; the third and final volume is forthcoming. Bolsterli is also the editor of the University of Arkansas Press's *Vinegar Pie and Chicken Bread* and *A Remembrance of Eden*. She is professor emerita of English at the University of Arkansas, Fayetteville.